REMOVING
THE
MASKS
THAT BIND US

Also by John Randolph Price

<u>Books</u>

The Abundance Book
The Alchemist's Handbook
*Angel Energy
*The Angels Within Us
Empowerment
The Jesus Code
*Living a Life of Joy
The Love Book
The Meditation Book
Practical Spirituality
A Spiritual Philosophy for the New World
The Success Book
The Superbeings
The Wellness Book
With Wings As Eagles
The Workbook for Self-Mastery

Selected audiocassettes are also available from Hay House

Check your bookstore for the books listed above. All items except
those with asterisks can be ordered through Hay House:
800-654-5126 • 800-650-5115 (fax)

Please visit the Hay House Website at: **hayhouse.com** and
John Randolph Price's Website at: **quartus.org**

REMOVING
THE
MASKS
THAT BIND US

JOHN
RANDOLPH
PRICE

Hay House, Inc.
Carlsbad, California • Sydney, Australia

Published and distributed in the United States by: Hay House, Inc., P.O. Box 5100, Carlsbad, CA 92018-5100 • (800) 654-5126 • (800) 650-5115 (fax)

Editorial: Jill Kramer • *Design:* Jenny Richards

Library of Congress Cataloging-in-Publication Data

Price, John Randolph.
    Removing the masks that bind us / John Randolph Price.
        p. cm.
    Includes bibliographical references.
    ISBN 1-56170-672-8 (trade paper)
    1. Spiritual life. 2. Masks–Miscellanea. I. Title.

BL624 .P755 2001
299'.93—dc21   00-058097

ISBN 1-56170-672-8

04 03 02 01   4 3 2 1
1st printing, February 2001

Printed in Canada

*This book is dedicated to
my wife, Jan,
whose genuineness is
a daily reminder
to me that without
the masks that bind us,
life becomes a joyful,
fun-filled adventure.*

CONTENTS

*"Every man is a divinity in disguise,
a god playing the fool."*

— Ralph Waldo Emerson

INTRODUCTION

In the fall of 1998, my wife, Jan, and I attended a masked ball. The band played the delightful swinging-swaying music of the '40s, and we danced most of the numbers and had a marvelous time. I was especially intrigued by the variety of masks—some grotesque, others classic—and during the course of the night, I began to wonder about the "natural appearance" of certain men and women.

When the masks were removed later in the evening, I discovered what seemed to be additional false faces that had been hiding behind the masks—faces made visible by spoken words, telltale eyes, mouths set in silent expression, and physical posturing. Of course, beyond that level of falsity is the light of the true or higher self, but my fascination at this point was on the mask behind the mask, the "disguises" being presented as personal identities. It's true that what you see in someone else you can also see in yourself—particularly if a negative reaction is triggered. However, in this case, I was not passing critical judgment. Rather, I looked upon this as an exercise in detached observation, a study that might someday find its way into a book that could help us all remove our masks.

Noticing and overhearing the couples at adjacent tables, and listening to the men and women at the bar, and the guys in the men's room, I could see particular energies combining and playing together to put on a false face, one quite different from the true identity of the individual. I spotted the Victim (sufferer) and the Meddler (big nuisance), and then Jan and I wondered if we were playing the part of the Prideful (prancy peacocks) on the dance floor as the crowd watched our sinuous performance. We decided later that we were just having fun.

Now before I go any further, let me explain that the masks we wear are simply veils that we have chosen to hide behind in order "to get our way," or to demonstrate how we are reacting to the powers and forces that seem to influence us from the external world. They are part of our self-image, and in some cases, such as the Tyrant (bully) and the Fanatic (zealot), the mask is nothing more than a protective device, a defense mechanism.

In the weeks following the masked ball, I began to do some personal research to determine the basic or elementary masks that we wear. My initial means of inquiry was to discuss the planetary influences with our friend Coe Savage, an esoteric astrologer, followed by a review of archetypical energies from my previous writings, and then to probe my own deep consciousness for the universal masks from mythology. I also looked closely at the e-mails and letters I had received, put together profiles of distant relatives and friends along the way, and asked members of the Quartus Society (the membership organization of The Quartus Foundation) to describe the masks they had worn. The next step was to review my own masks, including those I had donned during my 25 years in the advertising and public relations fields.

In the course of my continuing research, I discovered—in addition to those already mentioned—the Manipulator (schemer); the Abandoned (have I been forsaken?); the Opinionated (know-it-all); the Worrier (if anything can go wrong, it will); the Yielder (I'll do *anything* to please you); the Obsessed (totally hung up); and the Deceiver (great pretender), for a total of 12 masks. There may be more, but I consider these to be the Big Ones. And even though we may not be playing the part to the extreme (the tunnel-visioned Fanatic can become a Terrorist), there's enough energy from the 12 masks residing in all of us to make life very unpleasant if we don't consciously take control.

I should also mention that if we're having sticky problems with our physical system, or menacing challenges in the relationship, finance, or career areas, it means that we have, perhaps unconsciously, made the decision to live in the lower or afflicted aspects of our nature. Maybe we think there's a lesson there—that there is value in experiencing something that makes us crawl around in thorns on cursed ground, or a benefit in submitting to suffering because that could be our ticket to salvation. Let's get real.

I've found over the years that if I really want a lesson in life—to learn what truth really is—the best way is to stand tall and face the music, the music being the understanding that my world is nothing more than the projection of my thoughts, and if I want a different world, I must change my mind. When we realize that the world has no power over us—that the power is within us—the inner Teacher takes over, we shed our disguises, and the "curriculum of life" becomes a joyful experience.

What influences us to wear these unpleasant masks? To expand on what I said earlier, a part of it has to do with the planetary energies that are impacting us from birth to the time of transition and how we are responding to them. We should also consider the archetypes that are a part of the collective unconscious that we all share—those forces that I wrote about in my book *The Angels Within Us*[1]—the energies that attach themselves to us and project as a certain form of behavior. Then there are the universal images that are hidden in the deepest recesses of our psyche, a part of the mythological lore that offers symbolic portraits of our masked identity. And finally, we look to the persona we are presenting to the world based on past experiences and conditioning. When the afflicted energies, forces, and influences are combined and operating as a particular mask, we will always have a need for an adversary. Why? Because in one way or another, these are all combat masks, and it takes two to tangle.

Can we take the masks off and reveal who we really are? Certainly, and that's the primary purpose of this book. You see, whatever identity we may be portraying, it is one that we've chosen. No one decides for us. In essence, we create our own experiences by the masks we have elected to wear. If life is filled with suffering, sorrow, conflict, and chaos, it only means that we have chosen those particular masks. But remember, *they are removable.*

Let's also keep in mind that there are higher and lower aspects of both the planetary energies and the causal powers we call archetypes. In mythology, we have the metaphorical aspects of our nature, but they are there to help us understand ourselves in our search for truth. And personality-wise, we have the ego, also called the Dweller on the Threshold, which represents the sum-total of the forces of our lower nature. But the Dweller is simply a mirror for us to see the personality characteristics that must be conquered—not an evil thing, but part of our road map to freedom.

There is a possibility that you won't recognize yourself as wearing any of the masks that are discussed in the chapters to follow. "That's not me" will be a frequent disclaimer—and then you'll think of and point the finger at a family member, romantic interest, friend, or co-worker. That is called *denial* and/or *identity transference.* Remember, if you see something in others that causes an emotional reaction, that negative characteristic is an integral part of yourself.

To help you get around the ego's protective games, I will show you examples of the masks I've worn, which may trigger a response in you. And together we'll strip away those false faces and see each other as we really are—loving and loved, joyous, peaceful, and totally fulfilled superbeings created by God to continue the creative process from heaven to earth.

Life itself can be a ball, when we toss away the masks.

chapter
one

THE VICTIM

I imagine that all of us at one time or another have donned the Victim mask. I did during the first grade when the kids began teasing me about my skinny legs. The taunts embarrassed me, but I quickly found the perfect way to squelch them. I stopped wearing short pants.

As we grow and mature, we can slip on the Victim mask when we feel our self-worth dipping below the norm, perhaps through some form of rejection or attack—or the inability to deal with a particular situation in the family arena or workplace. Fortunately, if we've made a firm commitment to spiritual principles and have an understanding of cause and effect, we know that we can change our mind, see the situation differently, and release ourselves from the problem.

Martha put on the Victim mask when she felt that there was nothing she could do to meet her boss's rigid expectations. He criticized her for incomplete reports, for hiring what he considered an incompetent secretary, and for being late one morning because of car trouble. He was the exacting taskmaster, and Martha, as she put it, was "the loser." After one particularly bombastic episode—she couldn't be found when he called from a client meeting the day before—she felt that she had reached the end of her rope. She returned to her office, closed the door, and prayed. She immediately heard, "Agree with your adversary." *No way,* she thought. Again she heard the words in her mind, "Agree with your adversary."

Martha gathered her courage and went back to her boss's office. She told him that she was sorry that her work was not deemed satisfactory in his eyes, that she would try to do better, but if he would prefer, she would resign and seek another position elsewhere.

The man stared at her for a moment, then in a quiet voice told Martha about the problems he was having at home—and that he realized he was taking out his problems on her. He not only apologized for his behavior, but asked her forgiveness. The masks of the Victim and the Victimizer had been removed.

Martha had followed her inner guidance—she had asked and she had received. But when a feeling of complete helplessness engulfs a person, reinforcing a long-held belief that he or she is not treated fairly by others, then the adversarial relationship of Victim and Victimizer is established, and the individual may go through life casting the blame "out there"—on someone else—to justify personal suffering.

Carl put on the Victim mask early in life. He grew up in a broken home, blamed his mother for all the disadvantages he experienced, and left school when he was 15 to get a job. He was married three times, all of the marriages ending in divorce, with the women always being at fault in his mind. He did have a son by his first wife, but Carl seldom visited the boy during the growing-up years, and a true father-son relationship was late in blooming.

Carl was now living alone in a garage apartment in a small midwestern town, working six days a week at the local hardware store. He had few friends and little social life, but he was considered an honest and dependable employee. When the store's owner decided to retire, he helped Carl buy the store by arranging a bank loan. Carl was in his early fifties at the time, and he considered this his chance to make something of his life—a dream come true. But according to his son Joe, "Everything soon fell apart. He was forced out of business when a giant discount outlet moved into town. That's when the drinking started. He closed the store and declared bankruptcy; and in the subsequent turn of events, totaled his car, landed in the hospital, ran out of money, and was forced to ask me for help."

Joe, now married and living in California, invited his father to move in with him until he could get back on his feet. Having been on the spiritual path for a number of years, Joe knew that every disadvantage could be turned into a greater advantage. He gave Carl a metaphysical book to read—"he was reluctant at first"—and then spent time each day talking to him (not lecturing) about the power of the mind when aligned with the spirit within.

Joe wrote, "Dad became more and more receptive. He read every spiritual book I had in the house, and began to realize that what had happened to him he had drawn to himself through his negative thinking."

In time, Carl became a new man with renewed self-esteem. He found a local job with the same national discount store that he had cursed back in the Midwest, bought a car, moved into a new apartment complex, and according to Joe, he's now dating a lovely woman—all within the past year. With the loving assistance of his son, Carl no longer sees himself as the victim of a cruel world.

Now let's look at another Victim mask—the case history of Rita. She had cried herself to sleep after a party with family and friends during the Christmas holidays. Earlier that evening, she glanced at her two aunts—sitting on the sofa in her parents' living room—and assumed that they were whispering about her. She felt that she could tell that this was so by the way they were glancing in her direction while talking. Her husband, Al, had recently told her that she always seemed to dress down so as to appear more mousy than she really was, so Rita decided that her aunts were probably talking about the old and faded jumper she was wearing.

Then in the kitchen, Rita's mother had asked, "Why don't you cut your hair? At your age, long hair isn't appropriate." Rita was 40 at the time. She didn't respond to her mother's question. She had heard it all before—from *both* her parents: *Why don't you grow up? You've always been clumsy. A little makeup might help, dear. You're lucky you found Al when you did. I thought I'd have a grandson by now.*

She walked out the kitchen door and sat on the back steps smoking a cigarette. She didn't feel anger or sadness—just emptiness, a feeling of being alone in the world and never measuring up to the expectations of others. Rita looked to the past, and her mind filled with the images of childhood—locked in closets for talking when she was told to be quiet, the emotional battering by her father for not cleaning her room, her shyness in school, and always feeling intimidated by her classmates.

Except for Al, who would date her late at night after taking his main girl home on Saturday nights, Rita had few boyfriends. She married Al during the summer after high school—during the third month of her pregnancy. A miscarriage followed, but he stayed with her. She thought he was as domineering and abusive as her father, and she blamed him for a life of unhappiness—deadened to some extent by her ingestion of drugs and alcohol. Two overdoses landed her in the hospital, which convinced her to stay off the drugs, but the vodka remained. After more than 20 years, Rita doubted that the marriage would last much longer and saw herself living alone, struggling to make a living. That was the case four years ago.

Could this mask be removed? It *has* been. Rita and Al divorced, and subsequently, a woman friend took Rita to a meeting of Alcoholics Anonymous. It was the beginning of a new life. She surrendered to a higher power, discovered God in the process, and began attending a New Thought church. With her computer skills, Rita found a new job and is now dating a man she met at a company picnic. Even the relationship with her family has significantly improved.

"Times are still a bit rough," she says, "but I've never been happier." Rita is no longer a victim of life itself.

The profiles of Carl and Rita are perhaps extreme examples of the Victim consciousness. Other more classic cases would include restricting life to only the basic necessities in order to remain as inconspicuous as possible, an inferiority complex coupled with low self-worth, and the fear of demands being made by anyone resembling an authority figure.

After I excerpted portions of this chapter for the *Quartus Report,* I received a letter from a friend and Quartus member in South Carolina who said, "I really identify with the Victim mask and have been removing it, only to find another mask behind it, like a first cousin. I call it the mask of Mediocrity. As I reflect on the past, I realize how unwilling I've been to go beyond *average*, never allowing myself to fully experience health, abundance, and good relationships."

I find it reasonable to assume that a Victim would certainly have feelings of mediocrity. Fortunately for my friend, that mask is also being removed as she is realizing her exceptional attributes and true worth from a higher perspective.

I also received an e-mail from a woman in Florida, who said, "Yesterday I had concluded that while I've certainly acted out and experienced many of the 'Victim' aspects, I hadn't actually worn any masks. But then today, one of those insights suddenly dropped out of the blue, and I saw that there is the mask of the Martyr and thought that maybe this is a close relative to the Victim. Life for the Martyr can be summed up as follows: You cannot allow yourself to win. You don't consciously go into the unknown dedicated to being a loser; in fact, even as the ultimate loser, you don't see.

"Contemplating the mask concept, I started to think that the Martyr is standing out there pointing up to the sky and saying, 'Hey, God, look at this suffering! Look at this terrible life! I'll get really close to the big jackpot, and just as I'm about to put fingerprints on it, I'll suddenly fall off the edge of the cliff. And to make sure there's no mistaking that I'm not going to touch that big jackpot/pie in the sky/reward, I'll make sure I fail spectacularly. Even if opportunity comes up and smacks me, I'll be loyal and true to this martyrdom.

And that's because you're a God who can't be trusted. Because if you *could* be trusted, you wouldn't have surrounded me from early on with people who kept preaching the Losing Game.

"So the Martyr has a banner, and on it is a symbol that stands for resentment. If you're wearing the Martyr mask, you resent your way in and you resent your way out, and the list of who and what you resent just goes on and on. You can say you 'forgive' individuals, but the reality is, you keep on resenting them."

She concluded the communication by saying that we must all step out in faith, not only to peel away the mask, but to also lay aside the old self and put on the new one, which in the likeness of God has been created. Yes! And when we do this, as she says, we will "be free of the rotten cloak of martyrdom."

And this letter was received from a Quartus member in Texas:

"Oh, how many masks I wore when I was young, just to blend in and not cause myself any problems: the Happy-Wife mask when I felt as if I were in prison; a Martyr's mask; a long-suffering mask. I went through them all.

"In those days, I wondered if God invented us out of a sense of the bizarre, or did we invent God out of a deep spiritual longing to believe that something larger than ourselves was in charge of it all? What I have believed has been dependent on what mask I was wearing at the time. Most of my life I've worn the Religious mask, hiding what I really believed. But it was almost comforting to believe that I was a miserable sinner (wasn't I already miserable?), a wretch in the dust, and only 'saved' from hell by Jesus. Yes, a sweet comfort, but with the harmful, underlying sense that I was less than something larger, unable to control my life, a big-time sinner for sure. My church created a person who was afraid to die, afraid to face a huge, dreadful judgment, even with the promise that one man had paid some sort of a ransom for me.

"So finally, in midlife, I freed myself from my mistaken marriage

and donned the mask of the Modern Woman, free to accomplish any-thing I desired, and free to explore other spiritual paths. I switched churches and soon met new, metaphysical friends who were on my same journey."

Let's look now at the energies that constitute the Victim con-sciousness, first from those conditioning forces impacting our lives from an astrological standpoint. We're not dealing with horoscopes here, and we're not concerned with the sun, rising signs, or moon signs. Rather, we are looking at the interplay of all the planetary ener-gies that influence how we approach life from the perspective of the Victim.

For both Carl and Rita—and others who wear the Victim mask—we know that on some level of consciousness they have chosen suf-fering as the predominant characteristic of their lives. *They are not victims of circumstance.* And with that choice they put themselves into alignment with the hindering aspects of the energies that govern the Victim. The result: misguided imagination and faulty insight lead-ing to emotional suffering, chaos, and confusion. Drugs and alcohol for these ego-centered people may also be seen as the only means to escape the turmoil.

Responses to life for most Victims are through their feelings rather than their minds, which produces even more emotional insecu-rity. Being overly sensitive, timid, powerless, and trusting of no one, they generally seek to be alone and are resigned to a life of separate-ness. It is in this state of negativity—particularly during the sleep state—that the individual becomes subjectively attuned to the astral plane, the collective emotional body of humanity, and has ego-ori-ented dreams that further enhance the Victim identity. Perhaps the dreams are not remembered upon awakening, but the debilitating energy remains.

The lower aspects of the inner archetypes are also highly active in the Victim consciousness. These are the causal powers within us that control conscious behavior, and if the Victim image is projected onto these energies, they will replay that misconception in the physical world. They will force the individual to live in an imaginary dream world (uncontrolled imagination) with wild threatening fantasies and deep inner struggles.

Fear of the unknown makes one stay only within safe boundaries, and if the person does step out to face the world, it is frequently done with an overbearing attitude and ruthlessness as a form of self-protection. They are suspicious of others' motives, and there is great vacillation when it comes to decision making. Such individuals prefer to do nothing until they're forced to take action, which results in much waste of time.

In mythology, beginning with Adam and Eve, we have the so-called reality of *suffering*—enduring life through the sorrows of the world, including Jesus on the cross. The symbolic portrait of a Victim is a woman bound by rope to a tree with a lion, a wolf, and a bear circling her. The key words are *"One who is bound to suffer."* Ponder this picture in your mind for a moment, and write down what you see. If you're an artist, sketch the scene on paper. We will refer back to your observation later.

Next we look at the experiences and conditions in life that have prompted the Victim's expressions of fear, anger, confusion, futility, jealousy, impatience, and low self-worth. The usual culprit is chaos in the family unit at an early age—child abuse by a parent, divorce in the family, death of a parent, religious fanaticism, severe financial hardships, and so on. Yet, case histories abound where individuals suffered through family turmoil to become strong, well-rounded *victors* in life. And there are even more instances on record of a Victim consciousness having come forth in individuals united in the most loving and balanced of families. So what was the cause here?

Psychologists say that personality traits are also the result of inherited tendencies, but scholars now understand that something "inherited" does not apply to that which is biological. Rather, we inherit memory-experiences from past incarnations that are bound in the unconscious. We literally transfer pockets of dark energy from one incarnation to another until they are finally dealt with.

Removing the Mask

If you've identified yourself as a Victim—whether in a minor or major stage—let's now start to remove the mask.

The first step is to become consciously aware of the spiritual faculty within. God cannot be a Victim and neither can God's creations, which you are one of as the very Spirit of God in individual expression. Understand this: God is not separate and apart from you. Your true and only Self is God expressing *as* you. In and around and through you is the one Presence and Power—the Divine Consciousness that constitutes your Reality. What you perceive as your "mind" is simply your avenue of awareness, given to you to be aware of Truth, the Spirit of God you are. And it is through this Self-awareness that Spirit flows forth to reveal a new life of love, harmony, and wholeness.

When you make the conscious decision to seek light rather than darkness, joy instead of sorrow, the hindering influences of the planetary energies weaken. The trend of life then takes on the higher vibration through a responsiveness to Spirit. There is no longer a Victim and Victimizer, no longer the belief that the world dominates you, or that effect is more powerful than cause. There is only life in the *Now* rather than the past.

Meditate, contemplate, and ponder on the truth that God is the only power in your life—a *loving* power that provides for all things—and that there is no other power "out there." God created all there is and pronounced it good; therefore, there is nothing but loving goodness in your world. That may not be what you're seeing and experiencing, and the reason is because you have let yourself move down into the lower frequencies of consciousness and have became attuned to the collective thoughts that fear evil and believe in punishment.

You have elected to live in the darkness of the underground rather than in the light of the secret place—that tower of light signifying the conscious awareness that God within is the only Presence, the only Power, and the loving Source and Cause of all that is good, true, and beautiful in life.

Understand that when you change your mind and seek only the Presence and Power within—rather than dwelling on the illusionary evils of the external world—you will soon realize that nothing can touch you but God's love. Then all fear drops away, and without the fear, you will no longer attract harmfulness from any person, place, or thing. Your consciousness becomes your shield of protection and draws to you only those who will love you and offer you respect, kindness, and the recognition of your worthiness.

Work daily with this meditation:

God is not separate and apart from me. God is expressed as my one and only Self, and I shall not look to any power or presence outside of me for my salvation. I look only within and recognize that every question has already been answered, and all that I could seek is already provided. I shall not want, for every need has been fulfilled.

No one has ever done anything to me. There is no power in this world to harm or intimidate me. All power is within, which means that I am not vulnerable to the thoughts, words, and actions of others. I am a radiating center of Divine Life and Love, and what goes forth from me returns in full measure.

I let my reactive emotions and conflicting moods be healed by Spirit and transmuted into feelings of joy and peace. I recognize the illusion of the senses and turn to the reality of the shining sun of Spirit within, the blazing light of my Holiness. I feel the harmony within and the harmlessness without in the external world.

It is God's Will that I free myself from my self-imposed

bondage and step forth as a strong, balanced, discerning individual with a healthy mind and heavenly feelings. I make that great leap forward now.

To continue the healing process, get back in tune with the higher vibration of the inner archetypes (angels) through self-forgiveness. Forgive yourself! In truth, you have never done anything wrong—it was only ego-action, that false self-image that miscreated, and you are now forgiving those ego thoughts. Bring everything up from the past, cast it upon the love of God within, and let yourself be healed of all shame and sorrow. Surrender yourself to the Spirit within, giving up everything to and for God. Then call in the causal powers within you and ask them to help you find the new Lighted Path. These are aspects of your Spirit, and by removing the ego-projections you have placed on them, they are free to help you be reborn in spiritual consciousness.

Take another look at that symbolic portrait from mythology of the woman bound by a rope to a tree with a lion, a wolf, and a bear circling her. What were your initial observations? Was it a terrifying spectacle? If it was, you were focusing only on the illusion of the suffering victim. If you look closely at the rope, you will see that it is not tied in a knot. It is simply looped over in front to show that you can break free at any moment. Also, the expressions of the animals are not threatening. They are loving and gentle, offering a ring of protection for you while you're bound in self-imposed captivity.

I should also mention that the mystics of old, the originators of our myths, said that there was an escape from suffering and sorrow through elevating the mind above the state of fear, and that this could be done by rediscovering your Spirit. What is there to fear when you know that the only Cause, the only Power, is within you and is *for* you?

Now focus on your exaggerated personality tendencies. They must be brought into your conscious awareness where they can be transmuted through spiritual discipline—the hour-by-hour practice of the Presence of God, and identifying yourself as Spirit rather than ego. Remember that you alone are responsible for how and what you think. No one else can do that for you. Therefore, what you believe about yourself is the manifesting agent for your experiences in life.

Commit these thoughts to memory, and drill them into your consciousness:

> *I have self-respect, for I know the Truth about me, and I am able to deal with every situation that comes my way through the power of Spirit within.*
>
> *I like and trust other people, for I know the Truth about them, and I know that they like and trust me as Spirit acknowledges Spirit.*
>
> *I welcome new experiences, for God is the only power at work in my life. I face change creatively and with great enthusiasm.*

So to the Victims of this world, I say, take off that mask of suffering now. Reach up, and in your mind's eye, see your hand grab the top of the mask. Rip it off and throw it into an imaginary fire. Do it! This symbolic gesture is of vital importance in peeling away the false face in consciousness. Now see and *know thy Self!* You are the Spirit of God, a Holy Self, and God did not create you to suffer. This is a benevolent universe, and God loves you and sustains you at every moment in time and space.

Rise up now and be free.

chapter
t w o

THE TYRANT

The dictionary defines a *tyrant* as "any person who exercises authority in an oppressive manner; a cruel master." Synonyms would include *bully, dictator, tormentor,* and *intimidator.*

Perhaps Attila the Hun fits this definition. He was called the "Scourge of God," and from A.D. 433 to 453 was considered the most barbaric and ruthless of the warrior kings. Then we had Hitler, Stalin, and other despots who later ruled in Latin America, the Caribbean, Africa, Europe, and the Middle East—all extreme examples of the Tyrant mask. But that disguise is also being worn by millions of men and women in everyday life—from the bedroom to the boardroom—resulting in a literal hell for those whose consciousness is subject to tyranny.

Early on in my career—while still in my 20s—I had the opportunity to work for a very domineering man. I say "opportunity," because it gave me a firsthand experience in learning how to deal with his bombastic personality and maintain a semblance of peace of mind. "Sid" was loud and coarse, with a temper that would flare up at the slightest provocation. Everyone walked on eggshells around him and worked in constant fear of incurring his wrath.

I discovered that for me, the only way to handle Sid was to display complete indifference toward his outbursts—to show that his anger had no effect on me. I wasn't consciously working with spiritual principles at the time; it just seemed that my best defense was not to return anger for anger or show signs of fear or hurt feelings. I just acted as if he were talking to someone else. By maintaining a poised and detached attitude and appearance, Sid's rage lessened—and in time, our relationship became quite amicable. At least until I resigned to join another firm.

Looking back now, I can see that Sid was consumed with guilt. Estranged from his son and daughter after having an affair with his secretary and then demanding a divorce from his wife, he was living on the far edge of emotions. To free himself of guilt, he projected it onto others; and to compensate for his feelings of self-condemnation, he criticized and damned everyone considered "below" him. His ego believed that in order to survive, there must be an enemy, and this gave it justification to hate and attack. Sid's religious fundamentalist background prevented him from understanding the ego's dynamics and what was going on in his mental-emotional system.

During the past few years, I have received many letters telling me about the battle-axes and bullies people live with—harsh, dominating women and cruel, oppressive men. One man felt that he was married to an overbearing "mother" who only found pleasure when she was tormenting him. They hadn't had sex in years—she told him she had *never* enjoyed it—and she constantly accused him of having an affair.

"She's got a mean streak a mile wide," he wrote, "and after 30 years of marriage, she's reduced me to a bowl of Jello." (Victim?) He went on to say that she criticizes him for his hair loss and the way he dresses, becomes angry if he forgets to wash his hands before eating, and then sulks if he's not hungry. He concluded with, "And Lord help me if anything goes wrong around the house and I can't fix it."

And then there's the wife who had to hide her spiritual books. Her husband had "gone ballistic" and threatened her with bodily harm if she continued reading "New Age trash." It's interesting that these violent moods also occurred if dinner was late—particularly after she had been out with "the girls"—and later when she applied for a job at the telephone company to supplement their income. Everything had to be *his* way—no compromise—and the mask of the Tyrant fit him well.

Lynn met Jack at a party and they started dating. She was in her early 30s, and Jack was a few years older. They seemed to have a lot in common, and after a few months the relationship moved into the serious category, with Jack beginning to broach the topic of marriage. It would be Lynn's first time to the altar and Jack's second, and when he formally proposed, she accepted.

A few nights later, Lynn dreamed that Jack killed her, and as amazing as this may seem, her father had an almost identical dream on the same night. When the two got together and shared their dreams, Lynn decided to postpone the wedding. She didn't tell Jack about the dream; she just said that she needed more time to get to know him better. They continued dating, much to the concern of her parents, and in less than a year, they were married.

Within days, Jack began to verbally, and then physically, abuse Lynn, and when a thrown skillet just missed her head, she ran for her life, called the police, got a restraining order, and promptly filed for divorce. She had married a Tyrant in disguise, and the monster appeared as soon as Lynn was legally "captured." It's interesting that she later became a counselor working with battered women.

Sometimes the Tyrant mask is softened to the extent that the individual is only overly pushy, irritable, resentful, and frequently annoyed. So where do *you* fit on the tyranny scale of one to ten? Are you touchy and testy—still an unpleasant person to be around—or have you achieved the rank of a true despot where people want to run from you? Pick your number and let's go to work. (If you're living with someone in this category, the material in this chapter may help you to understand the personality and perhaps find a way to help him or her remove the mask.)

Remember that the further along you are on the spiritual path, the less influence the planetary energies have on a personality bent toward anger. But if there has not been a realization of the God Presence and Power within—at least to some extent—there will be a vulnerability to the limiting aspects of those energies. Explosive impulses will be the norm, coupled with overwhelming desires. "Might is right" may well be the slogan for this type of person, leading to a brutish nature.

In the extreme, the Tyrant is hard and sinister, totally selfish, heartless, a power-loving oppressor blinded by intense egotism. It is a life of darkness and ignorance, with such strong emphasis on materialism that spiritual reality is nothing but superstition. Even in the moderate range of bully consciousness, feelings are repressed in favor of reactive emotions (a great love for revenge) resulting in little self-control. He or she becomes (or seeks to be) the dictator-warrior, ready to do battle when challenged. Perhaps in the case of Jack and Lynn, the courtship had not posed a challenge and he played out his mind-set in other ways when he was away from her.

If you've tapped into the Tyrant vibration and have suppressed the archetypal energy to the extent that those angels within have no choice but to play the same tune back to you, they will place an even greater emphasis on your arrogance and condescending attitude. You will be devoid of reason, possessed by a sense of your own power, with a continuing lust for domination over others. You'll live in a sea of unfulfilled desires.

Mythologically speaking, we see the symbolic portrait of a man captured in a cage and fighting with a sword. The keynote is: *"He who has been excluded from harmony."* Can you identify with this person? Look at the picture in your mind again and sketch it on a pad, or write down what you see. What do the symbols mean to you?

The Tyrant consciousness begins in the early stages as an organized defense system to compensate for feelings of insecurity, perhaps carried over from another life or from parental pressure in this one. The strain may come from self-doubt caused by a domineering mother, or repressed hostility toward a cruel father. Then, as the individual matures, personality differences in other relationships begin to play a part. A domineering man wants a submissive woman. A equalitarian woman seeks an equal partner. When the roles are not reciprocal, personality disorganization can result.

To this, add sexual maladjustments, security-seeking, and deprivation situations—and the Tyrant slowly emerges with a seemingly unquenchable thirst for power. This is power for its own sake, a need to dominate—with respect for others thrown out the window. To the Tyrant, no one has dignity; all are meant to be subordinated.

In the fall of 1998, I received a letter from Sue in California. She commented on some newspaper articles about "exploding anger" such as road rage, and asked: "Do you think that it is anger that has always been with people but is now surfacing to heal itself?" I put the question to members of the Quartus Society via the *Quartus Report* and received some interesting answers.

From C. in Kentucky: Anger is simply a cover-up for fear—fear of not being good enough or worthy enough. Fear is what religion preaches, and it is indoctrinated into everyone from the time we are very young. When we are feeling "not good enough," we want to prove that we are, and this can bring about what we know as "road rage," where the driver has to be first, out in front, and sometimes will even kill another who gets in the way.

Another reason for so much anger is that women are no longer standing for being controlled. World War II began the exit of women from their "place in life," and brought them out into the world of business. They began doing their thing in the 1960s and have never looked back.

There are only two emotions: love (trust) and fear (anger). The only way we can counteract the anger is to become loving and peaceful within ourselves. This sends out vibrations that others can feel subliminally.

From K. in Puerto Rico: *Violence is an effect of the frustration people feel at their incapacity to change their lives. We are living in such a negative world that it is a miracle we haven't exploded already. Thus, frustration starts to boil and comes out as violence. No one has taught us how to deal with it. We haven't realized that the most powerful weapon God has given us is our mind. Let's start using it correctly. We must take a more active role in changing our world, starting with ourselves—to think positively, act positively, and realize that the only one we can change is ourselves.*

From M. in California: *Anger is always present. A caged animal will attack. Often alcohol is used to calm the nerves, but alcohol also induces aggressive behavior. We can pray for peace on earth and think of large wars, but the small wars within the human heart should be our goal. We should pray that the mind and heart of the individual be at peace, and bless each human individually so that peace and harmony fill their lives. If we can have mass hysteria, we can have mass harmony.*

If you feel that you have "something to prove"—if anger is a frequent emotion—with frustration churning in your solar plexus at your inability to change your life or those around you, then there's more than a trace of the Tyrant in you. Let's remove the mask and diffuse that ticking bomb now.

Removing the Mask

I want to reintroduce you to a term that I have used frequently in my writings. It's *harmlessness*. I want this to be your mantra, your key word, the very foundation of your thinking. Begin now to monitor your thoughts, words, and actions, and see if you are *harmful* or *harmless*. There are no gray areas here. You're either one or the other—and you can tell by the effect you have on others and the peace you feel within yourself.

The first step in a program of harmlessness is to *want* to be harmless, and this aspiration will work wonders in cutting through layers of selfishness that have bound you. By practicing harmlessness, your self-control will dramatically improve. It is the spirit of goodwill, which releases the grip of the ego. And don't think that this will give others the impression that you are weak. Harmlessness is a power that will clear the emotional blockage and clean the mind of false beliefs. It is a force-for-good that will elevate you above the stormy seas of the collective mind and give you the self-confidence that has been missing in your life.

In my book *A Spiritual Philosophy for the New World*, I wrote that there are three basic requirements for attaining the harmlessness state of mind. They are:

1. **Poise**—the ability to control the emotions while fully expressing spiritual feelings . . . to be free from reactions to disturbances in the outer world while simultaneously being joyfully loving. It means cutting the cords and eliminating the pulls on everything that makes you feel less than a gloriously alive and happy spiritual being. It is the practice of "Divine Indifference," while maintaining a deep feeling of unconditional love.

2. **Detached observation**—to observe the activities of the phenomenal world with unconditional love and discernment *as if
you were not a part of that world.* This is assuming the role
of the beholder. You witness the Law of Cause and Effect in
operation as you see individuals and groups sow and reap
from many levels of consciousness—from the grossest to the
finest. You observe all without judgment, not labeling anything good or bad.

3. **Spiritual understanding**—to recognize that Self-awareness
is a consciousness functioning as an open channel for the
spiritual energy of Divine Mind, and knowing that this energy will transmute understanding from human to spiritual. You
become a mind aware of its Self, holding steady in the radiating Light of that Self, ready to participate in the action of
Self according to the understanding and guidance received.[1]

Pause here for a moment of meditation. Take the word *harmlessness* into consciousness, and let it become firm and substantial. Repeat
it several times, and let it roll around in your mind . . . *harmlessness
. . . harmlessness . . . harmlessness.* Think about what it means, to you
and to everyone around you. See it written on the screen of your mind,
and let the word speak to you. *Harmlessness.* Get into its energy and
listen. After a few minutes, open your journal and write what you have
heard and felt. Repeating this process three times a day for a week will
result in a dramatic change in your consciousness.

Now let's take a closer look at the Law of Cause and Effect, and
the first question I must ask you is: *Do you believe that God punish-
es, or has ever punished, a single individual from the beginning of
creation until now?* And the second question is: *Do you believe that
God ever rewards you?* The only correct answer to both questions is
no! Whatever problems you may experience in life are of your own
making and caused by your sowing and reaping. This is the law of

action and reaction—the karmic rewarder and punisher—having
nothing to do with God, but having everything to do with the good
and evil we send forth into the world.

The key phrase here is: *Everything I do to another, I do to myself.*
You may have forgotten this principle, but that does not stop its pre-
cise action and absolute certainty. What we give to others, we give to
ourselves. Explosive impulses return in kind, selfishness begets selfishness, and oppression in any form is reflected back as darkness.
Now do you understand what it means to cast the bread of harmlessness upon the waters?

I should point out here that when we live in *spiritual* consciousness, we are depending only on the activity of God in our lives. This
takes us above karmic law into spiritual law, where only harmony
prevails. There is no sowing and reaping in the material world.
Rather, there is a planting of ourselves in Spirit Who goes before us
to straighten every crooked place and perform that which is ours to
do. However, until we have made that assent into a full conscious
awareness of the Spirit within, let our dedication in "this world" be to
harmlessness.

To move further above the lower aspects of the planetary energies,
let's look again at the idea of forgiveness. If you feel any complaint,
criticism, or conflict toward anyone—including yourself—you are living in a state of unforgiveness. Unforgiveness means holding grievances, which blocks the light of Divine Consciousness and maintains
the squirrel-cage kind of existence. If you are willing to give up those
grievances, you can clear the channel for the power within.

Take a sweep of your mind and emotions, and identify everyone
whom you feel any degree of hostility toward. Now realize that they
have never done anything to you, that every reaction was based on an
action you had taken on some level of consciousness. Whatever you
projected from ego returned to you in the form of a person holding up
a mirror for you to see the cause-and-effect relationship. Now forgive

your ego projections, and forgive yourself for thinking that anyone had ever done anything to you. Forgive the grievance and be conflict free.

Next, look at the grievances that you are holding toward various aspects of your life—your relationships, career, finances, and so on. After bringing them into your mind, forgive them. Forgive the situations and conditions, and watch in the days to come how things change.

But we're not through yet. We also want to remove the blocks you have placed on the inner archetypes and free them to assist in this transformation of consciousness. And we're going to do that through the intense practice of unconditional love. You're working with harmlessness, an understanding of cause and effect, and forgiveness. Now it's time to turn up the love vibration.

Begin with this meditation, and even if you're not in tune with it at first, keep on until there is a shift into a higher vibration of consciousness.

I am love in radiant expression, and I send it everywhere without exception. Those who have rejected me, who have hurt me, who have not recognized my true worth, I send my love to you with no conditions attached.

I love everyone without exception. I love everything without exception. I am the power of God's love, and I let my love go before me to heal and harmonize every condition in my life.

Begin each day with loving thoughts, and continue throughout the day to *be* love, *live* love, and *radiate* love with all the power of your being. Then don't be embarrassed at the tenderness, compassion, and love that will be turned in your direction from family, friends, and co-workers. They will feel the vibration and respond accordingly.

And if that vibration seems to drop and you feel the anger rising again, stop and work with these affirmations:

I dedicate my life to Truth. I no longer look at my world through the illusions of the ego.

I let all negative emotions be transmuted by Spirit into feelings of love, joy, and peace.

As I give my life to Spirit within, I become a champion for good in this world.

I am filled with creative energy and enthusiasm.

I am generous and compassionate.

I am appreciated.

Now it is time to look again at the symbolic portrait of the Tyrant. Notice that he is fighting in a cage in which he has put himself and his adversaries in order to maintain control. But there's no one in the cage except a shadow, which can be defined as an illusion. So you've raised your sword to fight something that has no reality. You've been trying to use a power to overcome another imaginary force, and all the time there was no such force, no external power.

Now you can relax and put down your sword. Resist not what you perceive to be evil. Whatever you resist, you give energy to. Whatever you give energy to continues to live in your mind. But that's all in the past, for you know now that only Omnipotence exists—the All-power of God within you, and *All* signifies that there cannot be another power. Drop the sword and walk out of the cage. You are free.

Now look at yourself. The mask of the Tyrant is no longer there. It's up to you to keep it off.

chapter
three

THE MANIPULATOR

A Manipulator is a *schemer*—a devious, shrewd, cunning trouble-maker. He or she has descended into the lower frequencies of consciousness, thus becoming vulnerable to the side effects of the planetary energies. Under the impact of these forces, one has uncontrolled ambition for power, position, and prestige. These are crafty and calculating people, often snobbish and usually unscrupulous, with intense egotism and purely selfish desires.

The name of Grigori Rasputin comes to mind when we think of master Manipulators. He was a Siberian peasant who joined a religious sect, became a holy man, and promoted himself as a healer. In truth, however, he was a greedy, evil man. In 1907, he was brought to the czar and czarina of Russia to heal their son, and quickly began to exercise influence on the imperial couple and manipulate the affairs of government. To satisfy his thirst for power, he played a decisive role in political decisions, including Russia's part in World War I, and ministerial appointments—all leading to corruption, a weakened army, and finally, the Russian Revolution. Less than three months before the revolution, he was assassinated.

In less extreme cases, the Manipulators simply do not understand the meaning of compassion, and go through life intolerant of any ideas or views except their own. They will also practice destructive criticism, be prone to gossip, and be devoted to petty concerns, whether in the family or workplace.

Well, the latter part isn't so bad, we might say. After all, everyone criticizes or gossips at one time or another, and getting upset over trivial matters isn't that big of a deal. Think again. Wounding or destructive criticism, whether in thought or word, is from the ego—and to cause pain in another person always upsets the universal rhythm. Criticism is nothing but a form of self-praise, and one who gossips is truly a mischief-maker in the form of ill will directed at another through pride or jealousy. Petty concerns are simply a way to find fault in others to show how "good" we are. No, even in its most altered appearance, the Manipulator mask spells trouble for all concerned.

With ego repression of the archetypal energies, the manipulative person seeks to deceive, mislead, and defraud because the causal powers feed on the dominant tone in consciousness. They are subject to your mental-emotional vibrations, and that negative state is depicted by the reversed aspects of the Tarot: lust for power, rigidity of mind, emotional instability, power achieved through slander, egocentricity, unfair dealings, and so on.

The mythological symbol of the Manipulator is a smiling woman with her arm around the shoulders of another woman, whispering in her ear and holding a small dagger at her back. The heads of the two women are large, out of proportion to their bodies, and their faces are identical. The key words are: *"Unfairness is justified."* Capture this picture in your mind or sketch it, analyze the symbols, and write in your journal what they mean.

Myths depict the Manipulator as coming into notoriety during medieval times when there were few rules, and what we know as a social system was essentially nonexistent. Life was what you made it, and "anything goes" was the mantra. Fortunately, the universe always seeks to balance itself, and this cosmic interplay gave us the knights and stories about the search for the grail, which emphasized courtesy and compassion over treachery and manipulation.

It was said that the medieval knights taught us not only courage and loyalty, but also ushered in the age of chivalry—a civilizing force to counteract the manipulative brutality of the time. But as civilization progressed and we entered the Industrial Revolution, the Manipulators seemed to flourish. Human, social, and economic problems were the order of the day, with competition bringing on a new wave of imperialism. Enter once again the energy of balance in the form of humanitarians, enlightened government, and advancements in science. Yet the power and activity of the Manipulators burst forth again in the 20th century, and we now see that mask as an integral part of the human personality—at work not only in business and government, but in the everyday lives of the average citizen. This collective mask will be removed, and universal equilibrium restored, through a return to spiritual values in the mind-aggregate.

In mental health terms, the personality problem is the need to exploit others and get the better of them for personal gain. Everything is looked upon according to its prestige value—"what money, power, and recognition can do for me." The primary cause from the standpoint of early conditioning is usually the fear of *humiliation*, with the seeds of not feeling fully accepted being planted during an individual's formative years. This gives rise to a mentality with a distorted sense of values, and without some power or advantage to hold over others, the Manipulator may sink into deep melancholia.

Whether or not you recognize this energy as part of your personality, be assured that all of us have worn the Manipulator mask at one time or another—as illustrated by the following examples.

Many years ago, a friend told me that he smeared some of his secretary's lipstick on his handkerchief—and he made sure that his wife found it. His motivation was to convince her that other women found him attractive, thus making her more responsive to his need for sex. It didn't work. She cut him off completely, and they lived in a state of turmoil until they went for counseling, where he finally confessed what he had done.

While not as conniving as in the above situation, I, too, have walked the "influence deviously" tightwire. Back in the '60s, I was helping to plan the campaign strategy for a major candy company. At about the same time, there was a huge outcry about the evils of sugar, primarily from the dental profession. To counteract (manipulate) public opinion about sugar, I spent days in the library of the American Medical Association. Every word promoting the benefits of sugar was pulled from the reference books—mostly out of context—and when my research was complete, I wrote a "medically supported" White Paper on why sugar should be in everyone's diet. This became the foundation for a national public relations (PR) campaign in support of the multimedia advertising program. Was it successful? Of course. Did my conscience suffer? Hardly. The ends justified the means.

Today, PR campaigns laced with statistical evidence to prove a point are common ways to influence public opinion, as are "leaks" to the press. Read your newspaper and notice all the anonymous or unnamed sources who try to influence and sway our minds in a particular direction.

Jan and I have also known people who used gossip to hurt someone for personal gain. In one case, the causative factor was pure jealousy. Liz seemed to top the popularity poll in a large circle of new friends she had made. She was pretty, witty, and had it all together. This was too much for Edie, who had previously assumed the position of pack leader. So the whispering campaign against Liz began, and it wasn't long before Liz found herself on the outside of the circle. But eventually good sense prevailed, and Edie suffered the backlash of her lies in such a dramatic fashion that she and her husband were later divorced.

I've seen a similar situation in the business world, where men and women jockeying for a position on the corporate ladder would work covertly to turn people against their perceived competitor in the promotion process. Example: A department head in one of my client companies—considered a candidate for a VP position—spread the word that a rival executive was cheating on his wife. In that highly conservative company, an extramarital affair was a death knoll. He not only didn't get the position (the Manipulator did), but he was subsequently fired. It was probably the best thing that could have happened to him, though, as he was soon offered a job with another company, where he got a large salary increase and the title of vice president. And the Manipulator? He was later caught in a conflict-of-interest scheme and was asked to resign.

Do we find many Manipulators on the spiritual path? Yes, and although they are more benign, the belief that the ends justify the means still lingers—at least on a subconscious level. Also, the main emphasis in life continues to be "having one's own way" and "making things happen." Here's an example.

Neal had been reading spiritual books and practicing metaphysical principles for nearly ten years, yet he found himself taking an action that he realized was pure manipulation. He asked a friend to telephone his company posing as an associate with a leading management consulting firm (a headhunter). The plan was to call at a particular time when Neal was out of the office, and to leave a message with the receptionist. Knowing that she was the company gossip (another Manipulator), he figured that his boss would soon get the word that another firm was interested in him. The plan worked, and Neal was given additional responsibilities and a raise—but the guilt haunted him for years and negatively influenced his management abilities. He finally quit, made peace with himself, and found another job.

The great majority of the communications I receive from people on the spiritual path are highly positive, but in a few of those letters and e-mails, I've seen the Manipulator mask, primarily in the areas of pettiness and intolerance of other views. These people were trying to stir up the waters for personal gain, and it was obvious that with the Manipulator mask on, they weren't living a life of joy.

Removing the Mask

I am addressing the men and women who have made the commitment to live the spiritual life but still believe that some form of manipulation is necessary to achieve success. Is that you? If so, under the influence of the planetary energies, you have been using your mind to manipulate conditions and situations in life for selfish ends. The mind has been concentrating on personal gain with little regard for others because it continues to see and believe the lie of limitation.

Now it is time to turn the mind around and turn it within. A mind focused on the Truth of Being—the Divine Identity of the one Self—releases the energy of harmony and order into your world. Understand that the mind used correctly is a powerful vehicle for Truth, the Truth of abundance, wholeness, and success. Your mind must be transformed from an attitude of trying to make something happen to a new altitude of awareness of the power that flows from Spirit. Let Omnipotence work through you as you work with this meditation:

> *I turn within and focus my mind on the Spirit I AM, the Whole Self I AM, the very Kingdom of God where everything I could possibly desire already exists in all its fullness.*
>
> *My Holiness is my Truth of Being. It sees a perfect body. I now see as Spirit sees.*
>
> *The Truth I AM knows only lavish abundance. Knowing as Spirit knows, I am in tune with infinite riches.*
>
> *The plan of my Master Self is one of accomplishment and achievement. I let the great Architect I AM create a life of grand success.*

I am the channel through which the All-Good flows into perfect manifestation.

Then there are those who believe on some level of consciousness that the spiritual life is not practical for worldly concerns; thus, the perceived need for the Manipulator mask. Through meditation, you have been able to get back to living with fewer emotional pulls, but you may have accepted a belief that spirituality and materiality don't mix and that a desire for anything is a violation of spiritual principles. Therefore, you go to God for peace of mind and a perked-up feeling, then return to this world of form to do what you have to do to solve your problems yourself.

The root of this way of thinking is that there is no unity in spirit and matter—that divinity does not appear in form (money) or express in experience (successful career). Yet it has been taught for thousands of years in all the mystery schools and sacred academies that Spirit and matter are one in a "cosmic marriage"—and that what we perceive as form and earthly experience is concretized substance or energy, Spirit appearing as the form or manifesting as the experience.

I wrote in *The Alchemist's Handbook*:

> An ancient teaching tells us, "Matter is spirit at its lowest point of manifestation and spirit is matter at its highest." It was also taught that spirit and matter are equal because all is God, not as a reflection of God, but God as everything in the physical universe. Later, Spinoza, the great Dutch philosopher, said that mind and matter are the same thing. And Emerson was strong in his conviction that the material world is an expression of a spiritual system—that the visible and invisible were united as one and governed by spiritual laws. Then came Einstein with the revelation that energy and mass are equal, identical, and interchangeable."[1]

When you understand this, you will no longer have to "make things happen." The responsibility for your abundance, success, and right relations will be turned over to the Spirit within who moves from Mind to manifestation as part of the natural process of life.

Think on these thoughts:

I see in my mind's eye the radiating substance, the very Light of Spirit, and I see it filling my world. The energy of God is manifesting as money, and I now see money as a manifestation of Spirit, as the union of Spirit and matter on the physical plane.

The energy of God is interpreting itself as success, and I now see success as the accomplishment of Spirit. The experience of true success is Spirit experiencing Itself as success.

The energy of God is expressing as Divine order in my life, where everything is in balance. This is Divine Will-in-action for the good of all, and I see only perfect harmony in my affairs.

Let's look now at the word *trust*. Simply put, the Manipulator cannot, or will not, trust God. And this is usually the result of seemingly unanswered prayers in the past. He or she prayed for the healing of a loved one—and it didn't happen. And the prayers for protection and financial sufficiency fell on deaf ears, or were ignored by an uncaring deity. So there was nothing else to do but take control and work the angles as shrewdly as possible.

Bill wrote that he obviously put on the Manipulator mask when he realized that he trusted himself more than God. "God was only something that I had heard and read about, but had not experienced personally. Even so, my prayers were directed to this inner power, but when they weren't answered, I had no choice but to take action that I felt was best for me. When I followed my gut feelings, I often got good results. When I felt that I had to practice a little deception here and there to get what I wanted, things rarely worked out. Later it came to me that my gut feelings were moving me in the direction that I had prayed for, so I began to consider the possibility that maybe there was a higher creative intelligence helping me. I began reading spiritual books, got my ethics back in order, and began to understand what 'divine intuition' was. That's when I started trusting the Presence within. I haven't worn that mask since."

Another way to become attuned to the beneficial aspects of the planetary energies is to practice the idea of doing everything *for the good of others.* What you want for yourself you must want for friends and enemies alike, because in the cosmic scheme, we are all one, and to deny others is to deny yourself. You can free the archetypes, the living energies within, to assist you on the journey through life if you will pay more attention to your creative impulses. Find joy in accomplishment, rather than trying to show others how clever you are. Practice discretion, discernment, and patience, and strive to new heights of endeavor on the path of right action and goodwill toward all. Ponder these thoughts:

I now derive satisfaction from the simple pleasures of life. I have nothing to prove anymore. I can be myself.

I am able to love others and consider their interests as equal to mine, for we are all one in the universal family.

I am able to meet every demand in life through my awareness, understanding, and knowledge of Who and What I am.

Now we look at the symbolic portrait of the Manipulator again. Earlier you brought the picture into your mind—a smiling woman with her arm around the shoulders of another woman, whispering in her ear and holding a small dagger at her back. The key words were: *Unfairness is justified.* The large heads of the two women imply that mental rather than spiritual power is being used. Also, the identical faces emphasize the truth that what you do to others, you do to yourself. To scheme and work deviously toward another is to bring trouble to you, as shown by the dagger. Stop whispering (gossiping, critically judging), and drop the dagger.

You don't need the Manipulator mask any longer. It never brought you the fulfillment of your desires. Take it off now, let it go, and be at peace.

chapter
four

THE ABANDONED

When we think of someone who has been abandoned or forsaken, we usually think of Jesus on the cross, and his cry, "My God, my God, why hast Thou forsaken me?" (Mt. 27:46.) This record in scripture is obviously a misinterpretation, because Jesus, in the realization of his Divine Identity, would not have spoken such words. What the firsthand witnesses to the crucifixion thought they heard represented their own fear and guilt projected on God as blame for the criminal act they perceived to be happening. This was later cleared up by Paul in Hebrews 13:5, when he quotes God as saying, "I will never fail you or forsake you."

We have discussed a spiritually barren life in earlier chapters—when prayer doesn't seem to work—and that state of affairs certainly applies to this mask. David was wearing it when he said in Psalm 42:5, "Why are you downcast, O my soul?"

I've experienced such dry times, and I'm sure you have, too, especially when we feel our bodies, bank accounts, relationships, and life itself being cruelly assailed by the forces of "this world." We feel forsaken and blame God for not helping us in our hour of need. This is much like the Dark Night of the Soul, or the despair of the Prodigal Son when "he began to be in want." Curious as it may seem, this attack on what/who we hold dear—and the resulting suffering and sorrow—has its origin in the world of Effects rather than in the realm of Cause, or God. For example, the Apostles were looking to Jesus-the-man to liberate Israel, restore the Jewish state, and open the gates of heaven to usher in a new kingdom of peace—a total focus on personal power in the external world for freedom and salvation.

It also happens today when we are caught in the void of trying to live in the "neither world" between spirituality and materiality. We find that we are no longer satisfied with our lives, yet we are not willing to completely surrender to the only Presence, Power, Source, and Cause there is. Rather, we look to others to fulfill our needs—whether it be love, money, a cure for a physical malady, or to become more spiritual. And when we don't find the help we think we need, there is only a continuing sense of emptiness.

Let's remember that we have created our world with our minds, and that anything that seems to happen to us is the result of a decision that we have made on one level of consciousness or another. Perhaps we have unconsciously chosen a physical ailment to atone for guilt, or have taken an action that brought on fear, which has outpictured as a serious difficulty. We go to God to fix it and nothing happens because we're focusing on the problem rather than the solution. We want the outer condition healed without correcting what caused the condition in the first place. Frustrated with Spirit, we go to others for relief and we don't get it. A Dark Night, indeed.

Fred's one and only extramarital affair filled him with remorse and guilt, and the first target of guilt is always the body. What began as headaches soon turned into such extreme pain in his back that he could hardly straighten up. He prayed for a healing, but the pain continued. He felt forsaken. There was no relief from doctors either, except for medication that barely dulled the pain. Then one day in church he heard the minister say, "Error leaves no stains when we accept God's love." Later that afternoon, he spent time in contemplative meditation trying to connect with that divine love, and he began to feel what he called "a great calm." Then he opened his Bible and found the story of the adulterous woman in John 8:2-11, and found another shift in his consciousness when he read the last part of the story. Jesus asked the woman, "Has no one condemned you?" She said, "No one, Lord." And Jesus said, "Neither do I condemn you; go, and do not sin again."

Fred wrote, "If she wasn't condemned, then neither was I, except in my own mind for my terrible error in judgment, and I realized then that the error could be corrected through forgiveness of my moment of weakness. I worked for days forgiving myself and releasing the guilt to Spirit, and then one morning I woke up without any pain. And you can be sure that I won't have any more spells of missing the mark again."

The mask of an Abandoned one had been removed.

Julie's husband died when they were both in their 30s, leaving two small children without a father. She said, "Talk about abandonment! I was mad as hell at Tim for leaving me, and on top of the anger, I felt a terrible loss. As you have written, 'loss attracts loss,' and I certainly experienced that as a truth. I quickly lost the insurance money through careless mismanagement and had to find a job, which I soon lost because my mind was more on the children than on the work. The house was next to go. Tim's untimely passing had brought down my whole world. As you know, I finally climbed out of the hole when I stopped looking to the world of effects for my support."

Julie worked with our 40-Day Prosperity Plan to "make some money," and when nothing happened, she started again, this time carefully reading the preparatory information. It was this particular material, she said, that finally "clicked" in her consciousness.

Permit me to excerpt those pages (21–24) from *The Abundance Book* to show you the catalyst for the change. Where the word *money* is used, change it to fit your situation—that is, any specific "good" you are seeking in the external world.

Money is an effect. When you concentrate on the effect, you are forgetting the cause, and when you forget the cause, the effect begins to diminish. When you focus your attention on getting money, you are actually shutting off your supply. You must begin this very moment to cease believing that money is your substance, your supply, your support, your security, or your safety. Money is not—but God is!

You must look to God alone as THE Source, and take your mind completely off the outer effect. If you give power to any mortal as even being the channel for your supply, you are limiting your good.

The time must come when you will satisfy a need for money by steadfastly depending on the Master Self within—and not on anything in the outer world of form. Until you do this, you will continue to experience the uncertainties of supply for the rest of your life. Realize that this is the opportunity you have been waiting for to demonstrate the Truth of your birthright. Know that this entire experience is but an illusion, an outpicturing of your beliefs, an effect of your consciousness. But you are going to stop giving any power to the illusion, to the effect. You are going to cease feeding it with negative energy. You are going to withdraw your energy from the outer scene and let it die; let it fade back into the nothingness from which it came.

Take your stand this day as a spiritual being, and renounce all claims to humanhood and mortality. Care not what is going on in your world. Turn away from the effects, wave good-bye to external false-belief pictures, and return to the Father's House where you have belonged ever since you left under the spell of materiality. Take your stand and prove God now![1]

Now what does this really mean? The key is to depend *totally* on the Spirit of God within and not on the external world for anything—including love, approval, companionship, support, and security. For example, Steven says that he went through the Dark Night when his wife filed for divorce. He had depended on her for "divine order" in the house, a helpmate in business, and for his overall contentment and peace of mind. "That all disappeared when she left," he wrote, "and I spent months trying to pick up the pieces. It wasn't until I went through spiritual counseling that I realized that I had made my wife my god and had depended on her for my happiness in life. I'm working now to get my priorities straight."

Clara felt abandoned by her son. "After spending my whole life for him, he decides to move to another town. At my age (80s), you would think he would be more considerate." The idea of being dependent on her son was a decision that Clara had made, whether consciously or not, and as in the other cases, she was substituting him for God's love, joy, and fulfillment.

Now let's look at abandonment from another angle. Remember the example of Bill in the previous chapter? He trusted himself more than God. Mary, however, reversed the trusting process. She wrote: "As a child, I believed in God and felt that faith in God could move mountains, but as I began practicing metaphysics, it dawned on me that I had no faith in *me*. I believed that God could work miracles in my life, but I didn't believe that I had the consciousness for miracles; therefore, I negated the God-power. The books said that my world was a reflection of my consciousness. I tried to change my consciousness, but my world stayed the same, so I had no faith in my ability to think right. Because I had been a messed-up teenager, I guess that somewhere inside of me I didn't think I warranted God's 'good pleasure' or that I could be an instrument for his grace. I know that it's a paradox that I could believe in God and think this way, but that's where I was—in a big void, forsaken by my own state of mind."

Fortunately, Mary found the only way out for her: a complete surrender to God. "Through the surrendering process, I found the Christ vibration and let the 'human' part of me go."

The planetary energies impacting those who are seemingly abandoned are emphasizing intense sensitivity, egotism, inertia, laziness, impracticality, and impatience. The individual will choose to live primarily in the personality rather than the Divine Individuality, and the reason is that he or she does not want to seem different from others. The desire is to be "one of the gang," and not to be known as someone who is too spiritual or God-centered. And if the individual can't make it in the group (does not feel accepted), there is suppressed rage, with no interest to put into practice the truth that is sensed. By emphasizing the afflicted aspects of the energies in consciousness, the person will actually repel people, which leads to hyper-loneliness and a "no one cares about me" attitude that is then projected on others to play the part of the Abandoner.

Same thing with the inner archetypes. What you impress on them, they will express, and in this state of consciousness it comes forth as rigidity of mind, a reluctance to accept another's viewpoint, easily hurt feelings, and a belief that you are not judged fairly by others, all of which results in self-doubt, lack of trust, apathy, and lethargy.

The mythological picture of the Abandoned one is a naked woman kneeling on a beach all alone, waving to a ship sailing in the distance. The keynote is: *One who is abandoned to a useless life.* Again, capture the picture in your mind, and either sketch it or describe the symbols in your journal for later review.

A consciousness of abandonment may begin in early childhood with the death or divorce of a parent, the father taking a job in another town and seldom seeing the child, or perhaps feeling lost in a large family of brothers and sisters and not receiving enough attention. Other factors to consider are lack of affection from parents resulting in a high degree of childhood insecurity. As the child matures, all pleasure in life is seen to be exclusively in the outer world of form and experience. A neurotic need then develops for someone "out there" to fulfill all expectations of life, and to take the responsibility for loving, protecting, and caring for the individual. All the time there is an unconscious fear of desertion—and this fear is projected on love partners, family, father figures in the workplace, and mother figures among friends. This energy repels, pushes people away, and leads to that self-fulfilling prophecy of abandonment.

Removing the Mask

The only way to peel away this mask is to change your mind, and the first step, of course, is forgiveness—forgiving yourself for your miscreative thoughts, and forgiving others for what you think they have done to cause your unhappiness. They really haven't done anything but act out your projections on them. Consciously withdraw those projections now, knowing that you must change the inner before anything positive can happen in the outer. Then you become a sponge (consciously) and soak up the full Presence of your true Identity and let your Holy Self live in and through and *as* you. Look not to the external world of effects for your love, joy, and peace, but focus only on the world of Spirit within for *everything* in life. It is a complete abandonment to Spirit and Spirit only.

Here is a meditation from *The Jesus Code* that will help you move from a focus on effects to a deeper consciousness of your Source.

> *I understand that the effects of this world are from the past and are not creative. One effect does not birth another, for everything emanates from consciousness.*
>
> *I affirm with mind and heart that no person, place, thing, condition, or situation in the external world has power over me, or has the power to create anew for me.*
>
> *I place my total dependence on Spirit within, releasing everything to the presence of God I AM, knowing that Love has met my every need, want, or desire even before they were experienced in mind and heart.*
>
> *I am a Whole Person, spiritually, mentally, emotionally, and physically. And my world reflects that Wholeness.*[2]

Remember that your world is the result, or a product, of your thoughts, and miscreative thoughts can make for a hellish world. If you plan a project or take an action specifically to yield a particular result in the external world—without divine guidance or the flow-through of creative wisdom that instructs on a *spiritual* level—then you are serving ego. You are trying to create effects that the ego wants in order to fulfill its desires, and when the effects "fail" you—that is, they do not provide the harmony you are seeking—you feel forsaken. Maybe this was followed by turning to Spirit in prayerful meditation to energize the effects, to make them what you wanted them to be—to make people do what you wanted them to do. And when nothing seemed to happen in the material world to your liking, you felt deserted by God.

The problem, of course, is trying to find supply, support, happiness, and harmony in the external world rather than in the activity of Spirit. When that didn't work, you believed that by being more "spiritual" through meditation, your desires would be fulfilled, which was nothing more than a continuation of the previous thought process, an uninterrupted focus on the effects even while contemplating Cause. I know. I've been through this. I have placed my investment in worldly things instead of Spirit, and when I finally understood what I was doing, I forgave myself and once again turned my life over to God. In one particular instance, the peace that came over me was undescribable. *Behold, I make all things new* was the message, and I was then content to let a new bright and shining world flow forth from the love of God within to replace the limited world that I had created with my ego thoughts.

To work *with* the planetary energies rather than resisting them, cut the psychic cords on anyone who you feel has deserted you, and begin to love them with no strings attached—unconditionally. This means to stop judging by appearances, and accept everyone as they are—spiritual beings temporarily living in a physical world and adapting to the dense energies of the third-dimensional plane. We are all as one, living and learning together in our climb back up the mountain. As we move even higher in our *seeing*, we acknowledge the Holy Self as the only Truth of Being of every man, woman, and child.

Also, think about what you can do to provide a greater service— and yes, you as one single individual can make a major difference in this world. Think on these thoughts, not as something to come, but as a present reality.

> *I accept my responsibilities in life.*
> *I have the ability to come up with new ideas*
> *and make them work.*
> *I grasp new concepts quickly.*
> *I am creative.*
> *I have great energy and vitality.*
> *I am willing to face change creatively.*
> *I look to the future with joyful expectation.*
> *I am optimistic about life.*
> *I love harmony and beauty.*
> *I am compassionate and understanding.*
> *I can laugh at myself.*
> *I have intuitive wisdom.*
> *I live happily and productively.*

These statements will open your mind to new vistas, and the energy radiating from your consciousness will attract opportunities to provide a real service based on your skills and talents.

To remove the ego projections on the causal powers within, those governors of life, work on your stubbornness, possessiveness, jealousy, and your tendency to worry over nothing. Learn the value of empathy, cultivate a sense of humor to displace your irritable disposition, and stop making material things your exclusive goal in life. You may want to write down these points in your journal and begin a program of building a solid base in consciousness from which the living energies will perform their cosmic duties.

Look carefully now at what you consider the reason for your feelings of abandonment: the loss of a loved one, lack of affection (or even acceptance) from others, friction in any relationship, a sense of failure in fulfilling your life's purpose, financial insecurity, or seeming delays and obstructions on your path of life.

Now go back to that emptiness, loneliness, loss, and futility that you are feeling in mind and heart, and ask yourself, "What is the advantage of this to me? How is this less-than-ideal situation in life benefiting me?" Let the answer come to your mind and write it down.

Understand, as I've said before, that any challenge, problem, or negative influence in your life is something that you have chosen. No one else decided on it for you; there is no conspiracy. These aspects of life and living have been chosen on some level of consciousness; otherwise they could not be. Perhaps you didn't say, in effect, "Let this be," but in the fabric of your mind, you wove an outcome usually based on some feeling of guilt from the past. And this choice, although it may have been hidden under layers of self-hatred, insecurity, and unfulfillment, was made to compensate for what you considered a transgression of the law of harmony. But that law sees no transgressions; it simply *is*; and it works to lift you up rather than bind you.

Whatever that feeling of abandonment, look at it again and ask, "What is the advantage of this to me?" And the ego's answer is, "To atone for my guilt for causing others (or someone specifically) to suffer in some form or other. Therefore, I must suffer." Recognize this as a decision that you have made to pass sentence on yourself. Acknowledge it and couple it with the acceptance that there is absolutely no advantage for anything less-than-positive to be happening in your life. This acknowledgment and acceptance removes the guilt you imposed upon yourself, the sentence is lifted, and you can move back into the stream of the natural order of life.

Let's refer back to the mythological picture once more. Remember, it was a naked woman kneeling on a beach all alone, waving good-bye to a ship sailing in the distance. The keynote was: *One who is abandoned to a useless life*. The symbolism of nakedness to you may have meant guilt feelings and an inferiority complex; however, in this case, it portrays the person having stripped herself of all pretenses and restrictions and enjoying a sense of freedom in a sensual setting (the beach). And the ship in the distance? Look at the smoke. The ship is not sailing away; it is coming *toward* the woman. The symbolic meaning is: Her ship is coming in. While you thought that you were abandoned, it was all an illusion. In reality, you have been given every good and perfect gift—all that Spirit has is yours. Accept this treasure now, live with a knowing and feeling of *HAVE*, and return to the Father's house where the robe and ring are waiting.

God loves you and holds you forever in the infinite arms of Divine approval.

chapter five

THE OPINIONATED

Opinionated: One who has a closed mind—"holding unreasonably or obstinately to one's own opinion" (Webster's). Doesn't that describe most of us? Don't we all have convictions that shape our consciousness and that we express through our personality? Maybe the mask of the Opinionated isn't so negative. But when we look at it as the complete nonacceptance of the validity of the ideas of others, we can see where the trouble starts.

Since I wrote my first book 20 years ago, I haven't received much hate mail—only a handful of letters—but the minds that composed those letters certainly showed a total nonacceptance of my ideas. Then I had to determine how closed my mind was to *their* opinions, which made me realize that we all live on various frequencies of consciousness, and no one is completely right or wrong. Religious conservatives may think that Ancient Wisdom and New Thought were inspired by the Devil, and conversely, we may look upon the fundamentalists as ignorant or insane. Unless the mind is locked and the key thrown away, we should at least try to find our points of agreement, and then let everyone follow their own light or darkness. People create their own experiences out of the tone and pitch of their consciousness, and we should learn to be impersonal to the path they are following and not get caught up emotionally in their personal agendas.

Of course, this to-each-his-own attitude may be difficult in a highly polarized family situation, as Dorothy discovered when her husband, Robert, returned from a men-only religious crusade with a totally uncompromising mind-set. "He was a different man," she said. "We had been equal partners before, but now he insisted on being the dominant force in the relationship. He was the master and I was the servant—a role I wasn't eager to embrace, even with all the Bible verses he read to prove his point. It took nearly three months for him to get his head straight again."

I should point out that unless the person has become emotionally conflicted with total rigidity in the mental process leading to outrage, there is usually a difference between the Opinionated and Tyrant masks. Although a fixed mind can certainly become a bully-dictator, in most cases the mask is worn without violence. It is more like a pompous, haughty snot. In Dorothy and Robert's case, there was little anger, cruelty, or abuse. He simply believed that she had a "place" in the relationship that was subservient to his, yet he continued to be a dutiful husband, even allowing her to respectfully disagree with him. Dorothy's way of dealing with the situation was with love, humor, and what she called "intelligent reasoning."

Perhaps religion is the most widespread breeding ground for opinionated know-it-alls. In the fall of 1999, Southern Baptists distributed thousands of booklets aimed at converting those who are "lost in the hopeless darkness of Hinduism." This followed similar conversion attempts on Jews and Muslims. Having firm beliefs is one thing, but that gives no one the right to create an atmosphere of intolerance toward another's faith.

Then we get to the hell thing, the belief that if you're not following a particular religious persuasion, the doors to heaven are locked forever. At least the Pope used some "intelligent reasoning" when he said that hell was not a place, but a state of mind. A good friend from college told Jan a few years ago that the only reason we're here on earth is to suffer, that suffering through life is sort of like a passport to paradise. With that kind of belief system, bearing the cross becomes a way of life, and crucifixions in one form or another become an everyday experience.

Not all is bleak on the religious front. The Associated Press reported in October 1999 that the Reverend Jerry Falwell offered a message of reconciliation to gay Christians. He arranged a meeting between 200 gay and lesbian Christians and 200 evangelical Christians to create greater understanding and reduce violence against both groups. Falwell said that God wants his followers to love all people regardless of their sexual orientation. It appears that, in this situation at least, Falwell has moved from an unbending attitude to one of responsiveness.

Let's not forget politics. Have you ever watched *Crossfire* on CNN? Talk about bullheaded, unbending, dogmatic opinions. All is black or white. Liberals are bad, conservatives are good, and vice versa. That was the case with Cindy and Charles, where political crossfire between the two of them was an everyday occurrence. Cindy was a "military brat" who grew up in a highly conservative family. She couldn't understand the give-it-all-away liberal philosophy, hated any form of welfare or affirmative action, and distrusted anyone who wasn't a white, Anglo-Saxon Protestant.

Charles's position was the polar opposite. His father was a college professor, his mother a public school teacher, and he grew up with what he called "leftist tendencies" in his approach to politics and life in general. Cindy called him a pseudointellectual socialist; he referred to her as a right-wing bigot. They never found any common ground and stopped seeing each other after six months of dating.

Personally, I prefer the moderate viewpoint when it comes to politics. The liberal's emphasis on creative change, experimentation with programs to meet present-day needs, and an optimistic attitude toward the future is progressive, yet the reliance on government to solve all of our problems has created a threat to individual freedom. Conservatives, on the other hand, seek to protect the basic rights of the individual—to give each person the responsibility to choose the best course of action for his or her development. But this philosophy looks to the values of the past rather than building new standards for the future, and tends to fashion a society that is more repressive than open.

When we think independently, we can see both sides of a question or philosophy and don't get trapped in a mental squeeze of inflexibility. That's called being responsive to what is good for all concerned. It means being *thoughtful*.

Opinion comes from a Latin word meaning "to think." Having an opinion is quite different from being opinionated, where thinking shuts down and the mind falls into a deep furrow of obstinacy and prejudice. And yes, this can happen to what we call "New Agers." As I wrote in *A Spiritual Philosophy for the New World*, "Are you worshiping a particular diet as a way of storming heaven's gates? Have you, in your spiritual quest, become so spiritually pride-full that judgment and criticism are outweighing unconditional love and acceptance? Are your 'causes' throwing you out of alignment with the basic principles of goodwill and harmony toward *all*?"[1]

Back in the early '80s, two women left our workshop because I put sugar in my coffee. (Sugar and spirituality obviously didn't mix.) A few years later, a woman came unglued when she realized that I wasn't a vegetarian. And then at the Guadalupe River Ranch in the '90s, Jan and I were "lectured" to by a couple who were upset because participants at the workshop were able to purchase wine with dinner.

Spiritual pride can also lead to a closed mind. We have been in situations where an individual was so rooted in a particular spiritual discipline that all others were considered false doctrines, or at best, a misunderstanding of "Truth." In one of my earlier books, I wrote:

> Many people who have studied Truth for decades may not have progressed any further than a few yards from the bottom of the mountain. One reason is that they have found a metaphysical comfort zone that feels most pleasant, and after a time the mind becomes numb, the vision tunneled, and the feeling nature concretized. This "don't confuse me with facts" syndrome can usually

be spotted when an individual begins to be a bit dogmatic regarding a particular teaching, referring to it as "the highest" or "the most authoritative" or "the last word." Personally I do not feel that such descriptions fit anything yet written on Planet Earth, and certainly no person on either side of the veil has yet communicated more than just a few fragments of what could be called the Final Truth.[2]

In the Wisdom Teachings of all ages, it has been repeated over and over again that there is no finality of truth, and that any statement of truth is subject to many interpretations. What happens is that one becomes so fixed in what they perceive as the highest truth that the truth someone else believes is considered invalid or only marginal.

I've been there. I addressed this in *The Jesus Code* when I wrote about my life in the advertising business and how I chastised members of the staff for not using the power of their minds, with the subtle suggestion to think as I do. "I was preaching my doctrine of metaphysics, 'casting my pearls' before people who didn't know what on earth I was talking about and could not have cared less. Later, as president of another agency, I sent a memo to the officers extolling the virtues of affirmations and suggesting (demanding) we use our power to draw the appropriate clients to us. And the word around the office was that I had lost my mind."[3] Yes, when one is opinionated, there is little room for discernment.

I've thought of comments I've heard over the years that could border on the darkness of a closed mind, and added a few opinions of my own:

> *"People who are rich think they are better than others."*
> (Insecurity blended with jealousy, not understanding that the rich get richer by right of consciousness.)
> *"I'll never go back to France. The French people are rude and hostile to Americans . . . they seem to forget that we*

saved them from Hitler." (We always get back what we are projecting on others.)

"All lawyers are crooks." (A generalization based on a few bad apples spotlighted by the media. Also, it takes one to know one.)

"Doctors are only after the money." (Usually from disgruntled patients who thought the doctor was God.)

"Society is spinning out of control because of sex." (Something to blame for crimes against God, usually after a so-called religious conversion.)

"You can't get a good education in public schools." (Brainwashing from an extremist position.)

"The United Nations is engaged in an evil conspiracy against America." (Same as above.)

"The only good politician is a dead one." (Looking for a handout that didn't come; depending on the external world for salvation.)

"People hide the immoral things they do under the cloak of success." (An excuse for not making a contribution to this world.)

"Y2K is a secret code signaling the end of the world as prophesied in the Bible." (Some people will do or say anything to prove a prophecy.)

Add your own examples of closed-mind thinking.

Psychologists say that a closed mind is often the result of childhood insecurity caused by a dominant mother. Unable to express thoughts and feelings in an authoritarian environment, the mind begins to narrow down, developing a personality with extreme egocenteredness, more emotional thinking as opposed to a rational mindset, and with little empathy for others. Later, in adulthood, there is a neurotic need to control people by attempting to force one's point of view on others. The mind is closed to anything not considered "traditional" in society; emotional forces trigger disciplinarian thinking. Such a person may also be extremely materialistic.

Those of a religious bent may also feel that enforcing God's will (which they assume to know in great detail), or to change a spouse for his or her own good, is their purpose in life. They may also attempt to "save" others, which really means forcing their religious beliefs on them. This is arrogance in its most extreme expression.

Mythologically, we see a man with teeth clenched, eyes wide, while pointing his finger and shaking his head no. The keynote is: *"He who is held prisoner by his own thoughts."* Sketch the picture or write in your journal what you see.

The planetary energies that continually radiate upon and through us are of a benevolent nature, but the Opinionated ones have resisted them and have fought impulses that are welling up from within, thus moving out of alignment with their positive forces. Their minds focus on the possibility of loss leading to a feeling of inadequacy, yet a desire to dominate those around them is a powerful element in consciousness. He or she is a "head" person, with little reliance on the heart or feeling nature; the emphasis is on the masculine energy rather than the feminine. They live principally in their desires, which control the personality.

A know-it-all attitude also severely blocks the inner archetypes, and when their energy is repressed, the individual may become—perhaps without realizing it—an oppressor, a teacher of false doctrines, or a distorter of truth. The personality becomes unyielding, stubborn, inflexible, vain, and pretentious.

After running excerpts from this chapter for an article in *The Quartus Report*, I heard from a member in the Midwest. She wrote: "I was so moved by your article that I called my sister to read parts of it. I asked her to identify the siblings she thought it described, and she came up with an older brother who fits the clenched teeth description to a 'T'—and also a younger sister. The brother is the classic representation of the Opinionated mask. He is an elder in a strict

Bible (as the only authority) church, and has worked diligently all of his adult life to get everyone he meets to conform to his thinking, which is always 'RIGHT.' Fortunately, he has never resorted to violence (that I know of), and always uses persuasion and verbal 'nailing you to the wall' to get his point across. He is the oldest in our family and has always used this position of first-born authority. However, I see him as basically scared and crying out for love, and I'm going to send him your article with a loving note."

Removing the Mask

If you are living with an opinionated individual, adopt the attitude for yourself that you are detached from such silliness—that you are your own person with a mind of your own, and you don't have to be dominated by someone else's thinking. Keep reminding yourself not to be caught up in another's self-righteous behavior and inner struggles. That's *their* experience, not yours. So be yourself, and above all, don't argue or be defensive. With love in your heart, work with gentle, reasonable persuasion and appeal to the feeling nature. When the person realizes that you are not buying into his/her particular agenda, you will see a softening of the rigid mind-set. If this doesn't occur right away, continue to pour love into the situation, always working from the Spiritual Self within. Be the Shining Sun of love, peace, and harmony.

I also remembered something that H. Emilie Cady wrote in *Lessons in Truth*:

> Some years ago I found myself under a sense of bondage to a strong, aggressive personality with whom, externally, I had been quite intimately associated for several months.
>
> After vainly trying for weeks to free myself, one day I was walking along the street, with a most intense desire and determination to be free. Many times before, I had affirmed that this person-

ality could not affect or overcome me, but with no effect. This day I struck out farther and declared (silently of course), "There is no such personality in the universe as this one," affirming it again and again many times. After a few moments I began to feel wondrously lifted, and as if chains were dropping off. Then the voice within me urged me on a step farther to say, "There is no personality in the universe; there is nothing but God." After a short time spent in vigorously using these words, I seemed to break every fetter. From that day to this, without further effort, I have been as free from any influence of that personality as though it had never existed.[4]

If *you* are the opinionated one—and you *want* to be more flexible and tolerant in your thinking—may I suggest that you begin to ease your mind through the use of music and art. The ancients believed that soulful music and painting (regardless of how skilled you are) will change the polarization of thoughts and make one more receptive to the ideas of others.

I also recommend a daily ritual of working with these statements while contemplating the particular chakra:

> **Throat chakra:** *I seek spiritual understanding in all that I think, speak, and do. I speak only constructive words, and I use my power only for the greater good of all.*

> **Heart chakra:** *Love is the Essence of my Being. I love my Essence and recognize that it is one with all that is throughout creation. Love is the only power at work in my life, and I love everyone and everything without conditions.*

Humility is an important key, with pride and anger replaced by patience and forgiveness. It's also important to work with your intuition through meditation, asking to be shown the high vision of the great common ground between the polar opposites. This will lift you above the misrepresentations seen through the eyes of the personality.

Also, work with this meditation:

I look within to the Master Self I AM, and to this Holy Presence I say . . . I surrender my life to you now, holding nothing back. I give you my emotions to feel through, my mind to be filled with your thoughts, my eyes to see your vision, my mouth to speak only words of truth, my body to be the vehicle for your actions. And if there is anything within my consciousness, unknown to me, which is not in tune with your Holy Mind, I ask that it be removed now. I am ready to be clean and clear and in perfect harmony with I AM, my Divine Consciousness.

I AM perfect Love, conceived in Love, and forever aflame with Love. I AM the peace that goes beyond understanding, perfect peace in silent serenity. I AM perfect judgment, divine understanding, and active intelligence, for I AM the wisdom of the ages. I AM divine happiness, overflowing gladness, and the living ecstasy, for I AM the joy of the world.

The Opinionated mask can also be removed through a mystical experience, as evidenced by this letter from a beautiful soul in Louisiana:

"As a very young child, it was painfully obvious that nobody seemed to experience the world the way I did, and standing in the middle of the floor with my body, arm, and hand reaching up and stretching to the heavens—with the other hand cradling my brow—I would scream at the top of my lungs over and over: 'I am a rose among thorns! Why, oh why, have I come here?'

"Years spent in indescribable frustration and loneliness began to yield an unbelievable arrogance (I was the Grand Dragon of the Terminally Opinionated Club). Knowing that I possessed a uniquely clear and superior understanding of everything, if others did not or could not share these 'superior' views, they were just plain stupid!

That was my opinion—and I walked around in a constant state of amazement at just how many stupid people I encountered regularly.

"In February 1980, my grandmother died, and upon returning home from the funeral, I was alone in our apartment, seated in the living room thinking about her—about her life and about how time is marked in our own lives by the passing of another. Suddenly, the room began to fill with a mist. As the mist intensified into a fog, I could no longer remain in the chair. I fell on the floor with face and hands buried in the carpet. The Presence of the Master was over-whelming, the voltage so powerful that I could hardly breathe. The voice spoke, calling me by my first name, saying, 'I must have your opinions.' Telepathically I answered, because I could not speak. 'Lord, you are the Alpha and the Omega, the Personification of Truth. You are the Word. Surely my opinions are worthless to you. Why would you ask for my opinions about anything?'

"The response came audibly, and at the same time, within every atomic and subatomic particle of my being, 'You are indeed correct. Your opinions are worthless to me; however, they mean entirely too much to you. Therefore, I must have your opinions.'

"Brief, kind, divinely compassionate—yet these words cut into me like a surgeon's scalpel. This foul thing (not recognizable to me as such before that moment) needed to be removed. Those words, quick and powerful as a two-edged sword, spoken from the heart, mind, and mouth of the Risen Christ within me and around me, accomplished their purpose.

"It seems that as we speak less from the platform of opinion, our minds become quieted and our life experiences take on a different quality. We are better able to speak when appropriate from perspective rather than opinions—perspectives that have grown within our experience as we recognize and know that other people's experiences and perspectives may be vastly different from our own. We are able to step back and recognize how much time we have spent wor-shiping at the throne of our opinions—and just how much idle chatter we've spewed out into the cosmos. Silence truly becomes golden.

We learn the true value of speaking little and listening much, and as a by-product of Silence, an interesting phenomenon emerges. When we do communicate, there seems to be infinitely more substance to that communication."

Look at the mythological picture once more. See the man with the teeth clenched, eyes wide, and pointing his finger while shaking his head no. The keynote is: *He who is held prisoner by his own thoughts."* Look again. Who is he pointing his finger at? Himself! He's staring and gesturing at a mirror. The mirror image is symbolic of the ego, the self-creation that is frightening to him. He's trying to convince himself that he is right and everyone else is wrong. So in reality, the one with the Opinionated mask is fighting himself and seeks to be purged of his inflexibility; it is a cry for help. If it is someone close to you, touch his heart with your love, and help him find peace and understanding.

If it is you, relax your mind and realize that whatever is going on in this world cannot be healed by the ego. Give up your false identity as an ego-human, and let the Light of Spirit be released to do its mighty work. You don't have anything to prove. Be free!

chapter
six

THE FANATIC

Fanatics and zealots are cut from the same cloth. *Fanatic:* "a person who goes beyond what is reasonable; one who goes to any length to carry out his beliefs." *Zealot:* "extreme or excessive to a cause and vehement activity in its support" (Webster's).

I doubt that many Fanatics/zealots are reading this book. However, there may be a few embers of fanaticism remaining on an unconscious level that could ignite under certain conditions. Also, as the world spirals toward a major shift in the collective consciousness, we may see some disturbing scenarios of resistance and terrorism created by others. Knowing how to handle such situations will be important—and along the way, you may be able to help some extremist remove his or her mask. If not by you, then it will eventually be stripped away through a spiritual experience, or by the law of compensation—". . . whatsoever a man soweth, that shall he also reap." That which is in opposition to universal love and goodwill cannot last.

When we think of overzealous Fanatics, Saul of the Bible may come to mind. According to his own statements, Saul persecuted Christians "to the death, binding and delivering to prison both men and women." His trip to Damascus was to find those of the Christian faith and "bring them in bonds to Jerusalem to be punished."

Fortunately, he saw the light. Saul "died," and Paul emerged.

Members of a lunatic fringe are still active—perhaps even more so—in religious circles, and also as racists, political extremists, out-of-control financial manipulators, jingoistic patriots, anti-government terrorists, "rights" zealots, and conspiracy theorists, on down to the family unit where the mask is worn in violent behavior toward spouses and children.

A 1999 report from the domestic terrorism unit of the FBI said that militias and racist groups were acquiring weapons and surveying targets in preparation for violence. The report said that "those most likely to perpetrate violence are motivated by religious beliefs relating to the Apocalypse, or are New World Order conspiracists convinced that the United Nations has a secret plan to conquer the world. . . . The threat posed by extremists as a result of perceived events associated with the Year 2000 is very real. The volatile mix of apocalyptic religious and conspiracy theories may produce violent acts aimed at precipitating the end of the world as prophesied in the Bible."[1]

A follow-up report from the State Department warned Americans living or traveling abroad to stay away from large crowds during the Christmas season because of information received that terrorists were planning attacks against them.

Christian Reconstructionists would also be listed under the zealot category. They believe that in order for Christ to return, there must be a complete breakdown of society, and then a rebuilding in accordance with God's plan. Gary North, head of the Institute for Christian Economics, "not only hopes that America will fall; he believes it's part of his duty to bring it down, to be replaced by a Bible-based Reconstructionist state that will impose the death penalty on blasphemers, heretics, adulterers, and gay men and women who have had abortions or sex before marriage."[2]

And then there are the Concerned Christians, followers of Colorado cult leader Monte Kim Miller, who turned up in Israel. Miller "has cast himself as one of the prophets prefigured by the 11th chapter of *Revelations*—one who would be killed on the streets of Jerusalem and then, Christ-like, be raised from the dead three days later.

"Warned by the FBI, Israel spotted the first arrivals . . . an Israeli security official contends that the Concerned Christians were preparing for a 'big provocation' on the Temple Mount aimed at instigating a war between Arabs and Jews that would culminate in Armageddon."[3]

Fundamentalist Christians aren't the only zealots. In other parts of the world, a similar mind-set is also at work, primarily among Islamic, Jewish, and Hindu extremists. When you combine fundamentalism and nationalism, you have a fuse already lit and burning, and the drumbeats for a holy war evoke ancient fears and hatreds that are uniting the masses in a battle of cultures.

On other fronts, an animal rights group calling themselves "The Justice Department" has mailed razor blades and threatening notes to medical researchers in this country, and we know about the bombings of clinics around the nation and the terrorism against organizations such as Planned Parenthood.

Perhaps less extreme to the general public, but very real to the victim, are the problems of "intimate partner violence," with over a million cases reported annually in America. These men and women aren't wearing the mask of the Tyrant; those involved in beatings, shootings, stabbings, and rape have donned a much uglier mask—one that represents a fanatical behavior of brutality and savagery.

There are very few case histories of fanaticism and terrorism among those who are dedicating their lives to a higher power and are working daily to attain spiritual consciousness. This doesn't necessarily mean being more religious in life. Since the word *religious* often implies doctrinal authority, rigidity, guilt, and the necessity of suffering, I prefer the word *spiritual*, which means "the innermost" and "of the spirit." The Reverend Don Baugh, formerly the executive director of the San Antonio Community of Churches, wrote:

While we often use the terms *religious* and *spiritual* to mean the same thing, there is a vast difference. One of the key laymen in the first parish that I served as the pastor brought that home to me years ago. He was never absent from the services of the church. He supported the church by tithing. . . . He read his Bible daily. When his adult son returned home for a visit from the city where he was working, the man determined that his son had acquired the habit of smoking. He immediately became so angry that he asked his son to leave his home and told him that he never wanted to see him again. So far as he was concerned, his son was dead. His wife later told me that when she was expecting their son, she had some labor pains one evening following dinner. She went into the room where her husband was reading his Bible and said, "I am having some labor pains. Do you think we should contact the doctor?" His response was to shout at her, "Don't you know better than to interrupt my reading the Bible with news like that?" In my opinion, the man was truly a religious man, but he surely missed the boat in being a spiritual person.[4]

Reports of fanaticism that we have received at Quartus deal primarily with the alienation of family and friends over religious, environmental, and animal rights issues, where the extremist used threats and physical force against those not in tune with his or her personal agenda. A woman also told about her husband's Fanatic mask as evidenced by his abusive behavior toward their son at a baseball games—". . . screaming at [our son] for making an error, and later not only verbally assaulting the coach but getting into a fistfight with another father."

This isn't an isolated case of violence at games. Players of professional sports have gone into the stands to assault fans, and in other instances, fans have been arrested for raucous behavior such as throwing bottles and garbage onto the field, stabbing another argumentative spectator, and rioting after games.

Sometimes a person is in the wrong place at the wrong time. Elizabeth was attacked by what she called "a wild woman" in a New York airport. "I heard someone yell and turned around to see this woman running toward me with a spray can in her hand, and in seconds, my coat was covered with red paint. What this maniac obviously didn't know was that my coat was a fake fur." In the first place, we're told not to judge by appearances, and second, the action taken was certainly not beneficial to the cause.

We have also received letters about demonstrations that got out of hand and bordered on anarchy, with injuries and destruction of property. And as I'm writing this chapter, newspapers are running headlines about the rioters and protesters in Seattle disrupting the World Trade Organization (WTO) meeting. The wire services report that the demonstrators set off explosives, hurled rocks and bottles at police, and smashed department store windows. These were the violent Fanatics. On the other hand, tens of thousands held peaceful rallies to protest the WTO meeting. That was a *constructive* demonstration, which I believe can be beneficial in bringing about a sharper focus on needed changes. But excessive, unreasonable behavior and vehement activity is only counterproductive, and can lead to overzealous police crackdowns wherever there are large public events. For example, as a result of the Seattle riots, the Secret Service has asked police officers from various cities to undergo special training. Included are Los Angeles and Philadelphia, which will host the Democratic and Republican nominating conventions, respectively, in the summer of 2000.

Looking at the planetary energies that influence the Fanatic mask, we see that when there is a total rigidity of mind, primordial desires get out of control. Sullen silence is followed by destructively dangerous emotions. Feelings are inhibited and compressed until they explode with the fury of a vicious self-will. Such people are often antisocial fatalists, with a distorted sense of values and a pronounced thirst for power—believing that their ideas are the only right ones.

As the archetypal energies are repressed, a hair-trigger temper is developed. The person also becomes rash and impulsive, jealous and possessive, quarrelsome and combative. The mind begins to work against itself through a structure of error and ignorance, leading to a passion for disaster. An attitude of moral superiority makes the individual impossible to live with. As I wrote in *The Angels Within Us*, when repressed, the archetypal energies will "push those most vulnerable into fanatic idealism and fearful conflicts. . . ."[5]

Psychologically, the Fanatic mask begins with children who are unloving and self-centered, a carryover from a past life where religious zeal led to fanaticism. There is usually friction with the father in early life, and an overprotective mother, which outpictures later as a distorted sense of values and a neurotic need for power. Add childhood insecurity—and later, sexual impotency, a sense of personal failure, thinking more from fantasy than reality, and a belief in the salvation of martyrdom to the mix, and the bottom line is to always place the blame on a scapegoat.

Look at any divisive issue. In almost every case, the attack group that is radically militant and indifferent to the idea of harmlessness will be made up of people who are crusading against something that they have found in *themselves*—usually some form of guilt that they project on others in an unconscious attempt at atonement. The root of the guilt may be low self-worth based on their false belief in sinfulness and a worm-of-the-dust nature, or perhaps it is part of the collective shame of harmfulness that they have identified with and must be placed on someone else to relieve the burden. Thus, the guilt is transferred to the other party so that *they* may be punished, and so the attack is justified.

Clinical psychologist Kenneth Wapnick says that we see this in those "who seek to compensate for their own perceived inadequacies and inferiorities by persecuting and even seeking to destroy those judged to be inferior. People who unconsciously believe they are damned have often sought to damn others, even in God's name."[6]

Wapnick also points out that "the perception of a We-They world reflects our own internal split, as the ego pits itself against our spiritual Self and God. This split is projected onto the world where we attack the 'enemy' outside rather than see it in ourselves. Though it is often couched in socially acceptable forms, our need to find scapegoats to hate is overwhelming. It is frightening to observe our rationalizations for anger."[7]

The mythological picture of the Fanatic is a man with sword in hand riding a galloping horse toward a crowd of people. The key words are: *"One who will die to prove he is right."* Get a feel for the symbols, and write down what you see in your journal, or sketch the picture.

As I indicated previously, I believe that most of the people reading this book will not identify themselves as Fanatics or zealots. Perhaps you have been unreasonable or excessive to a cause in the past, but as your mind and heart have opened to spiritual values and unconditional love, there has been a shift in consciousness to a higher frequency. For you, I will focus on how to deal with Fanatics, and how to become invisible to their extremist actions. To those who are still carrying around a residue of overzealousness, I will offer suggestions to enable you to remove the mask—if you so desire.

Removing the Mask

First I'll refer to a passage in an Ageless Wisdom text:

> Lose interest in your personality . . . we do not desire to have fanatics in association with us. Arrive at it through a deepening of your love nature as it includes others and excludes your own lower nature. . . .You have to learn to be magnetic and to build and not destroy.
> Leave people free and seek not to influence them or to impose your ideas upon them. Your interpretation of them and of their need (no matter how close they may be to you) is not necessarily correct. Leave people free in all respects—with the freedom that you demand and expect for yourself.[8]

A master speaks to his students: ". . . we do not desire to have Fanatics in association with us." And the reason is that divine order is violated when we attempt to bind, control, or zealously influence another person. Such actions throw life out of balance and result in karmic repercussions through the law of cause and effect. So make the commitment now to *leave people free in all respects!*

But you say that you want to make this a better world, and you feel that through your zeal you can make a difference. Yes, one person alone can do that, but not when he or she is plugged into the ego and living primarily in the emotional seas of the astral plane. That's a dead-end street. On the other hand, when your focus is inward on Spirit, rather than on the effects of the phenomenal world, you are releasing a power that will right things in the collective consciousness with much greater efficiency than any disruptive efforts.

I can remember a business conference where contention filled the air, yet when a particular individual I knew entered the room, the environment immediately changed. He was the kind of man who always seemed to care about others. He wasn't embarrassed by showing love, nor was he inhibited about being a peacemaker in the corporate jungle. He was poised, confident, and sure of himself, as one who has found a deep sense of happiness from within. It was fascinating to watch the changes in facial expression, body language, and manner of conversation when he walked into a room. His positive energy seemed to work magic as heads were clearer, minds sharper, and the tasks at hand were accomplished with ease. A single individual can make a big difference—when the attitude is on the right altitude setting.

I also want to quote from a lesson in *The Jesus Code*, which may help you come to a greater understanding of what is happening in this world. Here are two brief excerpts:

> As the world moves toward the end and a new beginning, it will continue to mirror the illusion of darkness as the dominant force. Pray not to change the course of events or the cause of con-

flict will not be revealed, nor display reactive interference, for life must be played as projected by the collective mind, otherwise the just end will only be delayed.

The family environment, the communities, the nations, the world can only be saved through spiritual consciousness—not through verbal persuasion, religious conversion, theological decrees, political aggrandizement, or any other human endeavor.[9]

The key to this lesson is that the problems of the world must be solved *on the level of consciousness where they originated*—until there is sufficient light to dispel the darkness. And that includes the "causes" that you may be focusing on as an activist. As difficult as it may seem to the mind and heart, the only way to truly solve the problems is through spiritual consciousness, which affects the collective mind and brings forth the shift that leads to peace in every area of planetary life.

Where is *your* consciousness? If you really want to help this world, change your consciousness! And the first step is forgiveness. Forgive your concept of God, and forgive this world, forgive everyone—including yourself. If there is anyone you feel you cannot forgive, forgive your unforgiveness, and ask the Spirit within to forgive through you. Choose now to be free of any and all resentment. Can you do this? At least try. Why live life with undercurrents of anger, ill will, bitterness, and malice? We can never escape the consequences of our actions, so begin now to only cast upon the water bread that you want returned.

Remind yourself often that fanatical crusades are not in tune and rhythm with the creative power of the universe, which is love and peace—and this means that success cannot be achieved. There may be a moment of temporary triumph, but the impersonal law of cause and effect, of sowing and reaping, will soon reduce that triumph to ashes.

Safety is the complete relinquishment of attack. No compromise is possible in this. Teach attack in any form and you have learned it, and it will hurt you.

The only way to have peace is to teach peace.

Teach only love, and learn that love is yours and you are love.[10]

Make the commitment this day to teach only love and peace—and become an instrument for Spirit, rather than ego. A daily meditation on these thoughts will also help to remove the mask.

Spirit within, I acknowledge you as the only activity at work in my life and affairs. There is no other power, nothing that can affect me in the outer world, for you are the one force, the only power. None other exists. I know that you are eternally shining as the Holy Sun and the Light of heaven and earth, and I feel your radiance on me, in me, and through me.

Within the waves of your gleaming rays is the highest vision for my life. Let me see as you see, so that I may know as you know.

In the shining energy of your thoughts is the creative expression for my life where I may serve in love and fulfillment. Let me understand through your mind that I may seize this opportunity of joyful accomplishment.

You are forever extending yourself and appearing as everything I could ever need, want, or desire in this world. Let me realize this through your power to know, and be free.

Now look at the mythological picture—a man with a sword in hand riding a galloping horse toward a crowd of people. The key words are: *"One who will die to prove he is right."* You don't want to play that game anymore. The people in the picture know that, too. Look at them. They are all smiling, a peaceful look on their faces—completely nonresistant. Look at the man on the horse. You can see through him. He's an illusion attempting to be real, and the people know this and are waiting to embrace the Spirit of God, the only individual reality. Take off the mask now, and join the planetary family of Light Bearers, where the actions you take truly contribute to a more peaceful world.

Becoming Invisible to Extremist Actions

In *With Wings As Eagles,* I wrote about the inner alarm system. In reviewing excerpts from that material, I will use the term *intuitive nature,* rather than *subconscious mind,* as it seems to fit the situation more appropriately.

While we do not focus on the outer picture with any anxiety, we do use common sense and spiritual principles in protecting ourselves from negative situations.

And we do this by simply becoming invisible. Let me explain what I mean.

The energy of change that is coming in seems to be stirring up a lot of negative activity in many lives—and it's a part of the chemicalization process due to the awakening of consciousness. Also understand that the race mind is more vulnerable to the higher energies and is expressing agitation and resistance to the changes. The effect shows up in many "Phase One" minds that are closed, fixed, and unyielding. This brings forth a magnified projection of those individual's most dominant personality characteristics.

The energy of these people has the potential to create some sticky, unpleasant, and sometimes destructive situations if you happen to be on intersecting lines with it, resulting in hostile confrontations and other disruptive situations. So the secret of avoiding negative action . . . is to make yourself invisible.

Understand that the energy of every potentially negative situation is of a low, heavy vibration. If you have been faithful in your spiritual work, living your highest Truth and spending time daily in meditation, your force field will be on a higher vibration than the energy wave on which the troublesome situation is riding, and you will be "above" the lines of convergence. However, many of us are not as dedicated to spiritual living as we should be, so at times we may find ourselves vulnerable to "the snare of the fowler." But even those below the halfway point on the journey have a helper on the third-dimensional plane—their intuitive nature.

Let's say you're busy working, or driving the car, and suddenly right in the middle of what you are doing you get the feeling that something's not right. Your intuitive nature knows something is impending that the conscious mind doesn't know, and is asking for your assistance in lifting the energy forces above the level that the negative situation is on. If you will stop what you are doing and raise your energy above the frequency of the impending menace, you will be immune to it. The negative situation or condition will not be able to find you because it will be coming in on a lower energy level, and when you rise to a higher level you are no longer where you were, and the negative activity "passes you by." You have literally become invisible to it.

Since the attracting vibration is usually emanating from one of the three lower energy centers, I have found it helpful to start with the root chakra and work up to the crown in a process of transmutation, using either meditation or affirmations depending on the time element and where I am when the "alarm" goes off. For example:

ROOT CHAKRA AT BASE OF SPINE: *In the Mind of God there is only infinite Perfection, and everything in my life is an expression of that Supreme Wholeness. Nothing comes to me except from the Father. Only that which is pure, good, and fulfilling can enter my world.*

SACRAL CHAKRA BELOW THE NAVEL: *Divine Order reigns supreme in my life and affairs. All negative emotions are transmuted now, and I am joyous and free as I was created to be.*

SOLAR PLEXUS CHAKRA: *The Light of God surrounds me and I am at perfect peace. I rest in the green pastures and beside the still waters in total serenity.*

HEART CHAKRA: *Only the Activity of God is at work in my life, and God is Love. I let God's Love enfold me and care for me now.*

THROAT CHAKRA: *The Power of God is my eternal shield. I am totally protected by Omnipotence, now and forever.*

THIRD EYE CHAKRA: *The Vision of God is my vision. I see only that which is right, good, and beautiful in my world.*

CROWN CHAKRA: *I am illumined by the Christ Consciousness. I know only perfection and harmony. I feel only peace and love. I see only right action and joyful living.*

Continue the meditation or affirmations until you feel completely centered in the higher vibration . . . until you are invisible to the "noisome pestilence."[11]

Finally, what can *you* do to help the Fanatic remove the mask? The daily use of the World Healing Meditation would be important in impressing the collective ego. On a more personal level, love is the answer. Jan and I have proved to ourselves that when the energy of love is directed—with purpose of mind and fullness of heart—toward an unyielding, hardened state of consciousness, that mask begins to melt. Remember, energy follows thought . . . and with God, all things are possible.

chapter
seven

THE WORRIER

At the end of the 20th century, the Y2K computer bug seemed to be the most worrisome problem in our society and personal lives. It goes back to that old axiom that if we don't have anything to worry about, we'll invent something. Not only did we *create* the bug, but we also imagined the plague of effects: collapse of public utilities, malfunction of nuclear weapons systems, failure of hospital equipment, food and water shortages, crashes of bank computers—all leading to riots and chaos.

It didn't happen. As we rolled into the new century, we saw spectacular celebrations around the globe, with fewer incidents of a negative nature than previously experienced in crossovers from one *year* to another. The media reported "imperceptible" problems—"so trivial they won't even register on the radar screen," said a computer scientist. Fortunately, most of the people on Planet Earth didn't buy into the doom-and-gloom predictions, and those who did were able to "prove" their own self-fulfilling prophecies by creating their own personal glitches.

In Louise Hay's book *Millennium 2000: A Positive Approach*, she asked several of her friends to share their vision of the year 2000. Here is an excerpt from my contribution.

Each one of us will experience what we are holding in mind and heart—what we truly believe. I'm not saying that those beliefs will be played out exactly as they are held in consciousness, but fear will draw fearful conditions, doom-and-gloom thinking will attract that energy into personal lives, and the self-fulfilling prophecies from various religious persuasions my well stir up provocative situations for the "end times."

Even the ones who are holding their breath as we move toward January 1, 2000, in a stockpile and survivalist mentality—wishing for the best but fearing the worst—are going to find a sense of greater paranoia creeping into their daily lives. In one way or another, they will experience their prophecy of troubles.[1]

It happened. A woman I know stockpiled her pantry with emergency food supplies, only to find that her apartment had been broken into on December 31, 1999, and all the canned goods taken. She just *knew* that something bad was going to happen, and it did. Another person withdrew a large sum of money from the bank, went shopping "just to be safe," and somewhere between the bank and home, he lost his wallet. The leader of a survivalist workshop lost all credibility in his community. Merchants who promoted their goods with Y2K scare tactics found lines of people returning their portable generators, kerosene lamps, and other survivalist gear. These mind-sets had been focusing on *loss*, and loss attracts loss in one way or another.

The Ageless Wisdom texts tell us that scarcely a person in the world is exempt from worry, and that worry is the cause of all planetary problems. True, but there are Worriers of the common, everyday variety, and then there are *Worriers* of the chronic type, where the black cloud hanging over their heads just won't go away. I did a life-scan as I was writing this chapter and looked at the worrisome situations through the years. I've never been concerned about my health or my marital relationship with Jan, but I *have* experienced anxious times in other areas—such as trying to decide what I wanted to do in life (I had five different majors in college), and then after getting into the advertising business, not being sure this was where I was supposed to be.

There have also been worries over finances, trying to build a business, and later, the uneasy feeling I had regarding my books—whether they would be accepted and prove helpful to people. In addition, I've felt concern about conditions and situations regarding others, including the state of the world in the mid-'80s, the well-being of our daughters, the health and protection of our dogs, and my mother's physical condition over the years. And of course, I was a bit disturbed when the paramedic turned to me and said, "We've lost her"—referring to Jan's full cardiac arrest, followed by her near-death experience and her cavorting in the Great Beyond.

Tibetan Master Djwhal Khul said that "the increased sensitivity of the human mechanism is also such that men 'tune in' on each other's emotional conditions and mental attitudes, in a new and more potent manner. To their own engrossing concerns and worries are added those of their fellowmen with whom they may be en rapport."[2]

So we may conclude that some form of worry is a common occurrence in modern-day life, but we have a choice. We can handle concerns as a passing cloud, a minimal blip on our screen of life, or we can stew and seethe until things mushroom into a threatening storm. One way I've dealt with a worry thought is to immediately say, "Thank you, God." The intention here is to remind myself that whatever negative scenario appears in my mind is not the will of God—that God's will is perfect harmony—and my expression of gratitude is simply to affirm that truth. I also try to "tune in" quickly to Spirit when an uneasy feeling registers in the solar plexus. I did that on one particular occasion and heard the words: *"Don't fret over a problem that doesn't exist."*

What are *you* worried about? In 1999, we asked a number of people this question, and the answers included concerns about finances, job insecurity, old age, physical disability, violence in the schools, domestic terrorism, road rage, strained relationships, and family problems. (No mention of Y2K.) While the participants did not seem to be in a state of deep-seated anxiety and felt generally optimistic about life, we have met others with all the symptoms of acute anxiety.

Kate fits the psychological profile of the if-anything-can-go-wrong-it-will state of mind perfectly. She grew up during the Depression, and for most of her childhood experienced deprivation situations—inadequate food, clothing, and shelter—and from the "constant fearful talk" of her parents, she grew up afraid of essentially everything in life. This included strangers, going to school, men, social activities, and having to interview for a job. She continued to live with her parents and earned money by working in a nursing home. Her adult life was filled with out-of-control anxiety until she finally went for counseling, and with professional help, she was able to identify the fear triggers. She later joined a mental health support group that helped her deal with situations such as feeling comfortable with strangers, thinking for herself, and accepting responsibilities. In time, the black cloud began to dissipate.

Perhaps in Kate's case, and in others with severe anxiety disorders, there were early interpersonal experiences in childhood that gave them the feeling of being isolated, helpless, unloved, or unworthy. The failure of the mother to meet the baby's physical needs through rejection or indifference is unconsciously communicated to the baby, which builds the foundation for insecurity. In adolescent years, the lack of parental guidance creates a worry syndrome—"I don't know what to do." A neurotic trend of security-seeking develops and is carried through life. These individuals tend to lean on other people and look to others to help them handle their anxieties. They can also appear highly conceited—wanting to be the center of attention—while all the time feeling terribly anxious inside. They expect the worst, and when something good happens in life, they don't believe it will last.

For those who are vulnerable to constant worry, the planetary energies will cause the person to be swayed by every negative opinion uttered by someone else, resulting in a concentration on "what may happen." The mind becomes overly analytical and polarized in pessimism, particularly concerning material things. The individual is apt to be very self-centered, overly cautious, anxious about domestic affairs, and often has weight problems. He or she may also be a procrastinator, putting things off until disorganization sets in, which brings on attacks of nervousness leading to impetuous, irresponsible actions.

When the inner archetypes are blocked through an anxious, uneasy state of mind, they will become a force for agitation and dread. The person will experience a weakness of will, hesitation, frustration, self-doubt, and an inability to face reality. Tunnel vision becomes the norm, with a stubborn refusal to learn from past mistakes.

Mythologically speaking, we see a woman in bed, face tightened in an expression of fear, hand on brow, as the roof (ceiling) is caving in. The key words are: *"If anything can go wrong, it will."* Look at the symbols, and describe what you see in your journal.

Removing the Mask

The objective here is to peel off the false face of uncontrolled anxiety, which is definitely not a part of the natural order of the universe. While we may not eliminate all concerns while wearing a suit of flesh, we should strive for a higher plateau in life where worries do not control us—where we quickly think through them and get back on the beam of peace and joy.

To work *with* the planetary energies, think on these thoughts:

I concentrate only on that which is good, true, and beautiful in life.
I meditate daily to connect mind and heart, to balance my masculine and feminine energies.

*I love Love, and I radiate love to one and all throughout
each day.*

*I am in the Joy Stream, and every activity of my life is in
divine order.*

*I have moved from self-centeredness to self-awareness;
my focus is on Truth.*

I am secure in Spirit; my courage is strong.

*I am not overly cautious about anything; I am optimistic
about life.*

And to release the angels within to do their mighty work, continue with these thoughts:

*I place my faith in God, and not the effects of the materi-
al world.*

*My initiative is directed only toward success and tri-
umph.*

*I face change creatively, and I look eagerly to reaping
what I have sown.*

*The doors to my mind are open, and I am free to follow
the highest vision.*

A teaching from *The Jesus Code* says: "Nothing can touch you
but God, for God is all there is. What is there to fear? As a Being of
God, all power is within you as protective guidance, and around you
as a shield of security. Can you not trust omnipotence?"[3]

In that particular chapter, I wrote about the night of my firewalk:

A Native American woman asked each one of us to name our
most pressing fears—to talk about them and bring them to light so
that their darkness could be dissolved. When I realized that there
was really nothing to fear, I could feel myself growing stronger,
more in tune with the Spirit within, and when I walked across the

fire, I felt nothing but gentle warmth.

What are your greatest fears? Name them. Expose them, and then notice how insignificant they seem in the light. . . . The activity of God—*spiritual consciousness*—is the only power at work. There is no other power, and let all beliefs to the contrary be uprooted and dissolved now. God is our spirit, our soul, our mind, our *everything*. So what is there to fear? Nothing! This is a benevolent universe, a world of harmony and goodwill, so let's cease projecting ignorance and false beliefs onto the screen of life.[4]

It all goes back to where we are in *consciousness*. Let's remember that God meets us on the level where we are. I've addressed this in several of my books, but we should take another look at what this means. The Central Sun of our being, the embodiment of Father-Mother God and the Christ Aspect as Spirit, as One, eternally shines through us. This shining is power, will, love, wisdom, creative intelligence, light, substance, energy. It is the Allness of God radiating in and through us at every moment in time and space. And where is this radiation taking place? Through the level, the frequency, on which our consciousness is focused.

Think of a scale from one to ten, ten being the highest. If you are registering in the mid-to-lower range for health and wealth, for example, the energy radiating through that aperture has no choice but to express/manifest on that level, seeking the best possible answer-solution for you in that state of consciousness. This could mean intuitive guidance to see a particular health professional for treatment, or a creative idea that once implemented, could lead to greater prosperity.

God can do for you only what God can do through you. If you are in the pigpen, you get to wallow with the pigs; if you're on the mountaintop, all things are not only possible, but are fully manifest. Spirit is always doing Its part; we are the ones who limit the Great Unlimited with our states of consciousness.

• Keep in mind that Spirit sees you as whole, complete, abundantly supplied with every good thing, and living a life of love, joy, and peace—because Spirit sees you as Itself. This is the truth of you, but somewhere along the line, you have made the choice to see an illusion, and then worry about it. You see yourself as ill when you're not, experiencing scarcity and failure when you're not, and in situations of opposition and conflict that are real only to you. What Spirit is seeing is what Spirit is radiating through you, but pure light shining through a slide of imperfection does not change the pattern. It picks up the form and shape of the design and projects it into the phenomenal world as perceived reality.

Where is your consciousness? In the higher frequencies, we begin to see as Spirit sees, know as Spirit knows. *All that the Father is, I am. All that the Father has is mine.* But many of us sit around worrying and wondering why prayer isn't answered, why nothing happens with meditation, affirmations, and other "techniques" to relieve the situation. We let the tears flow and finally get down on our knees in surrender, not realizing that all of this anxious activity is taking place while consciousness is still in the lower frequencies. *God meets us where we are in consciousness!*

Yes, sometimes a seeming miracle does occur. What has happened is that in a momentary infusion of faith and/or love energy— brought on by our whirlwind efforts—we bounce ourselves up the scale. It's like jumping on a trampoline. We hit bottom and bounce up to a higher level where the spiritual energy radiates through at a new altitude, and even though we come back down, sufficient light went through "up there" to produce a positive change in our affairs. This isn't the greatest of analogies, but I think you get the point.

To rise into the higher frequencies—above worry, anxiety, distress—meditate on ALL that you are and have, and absorb like a sponge the fullness of Spirit. Think of a sponge being saturated with water, and get the same feeling within as you ponder the energy of wholeness, the light of creative accomplishment, the substance of infinite supply, and the love of joyful relationships flowing, pouring, and radiating into your personal force field. Absorb, absorb, absorb, and keep working at it until you are in the realm of mastery and dominion.

Now see-feel-know that the Divine Energy is shining forth, bringing heaven to earth through this new altitude of consciousness. And remember that attraction always follows radiation, the manifest good flowing back to you on the rays shining from within.

Keep at it until everything locks together in a Spirit-heart-mind connection. And these truths from the Angel of Success meditation will also be helpful in maintaining the higher elevation.

All that the Universal Presence of God has is mine, for God and the expressions of God cannot be separated. I live in the Eternal Now with the Infinite All, and nothing is missing from my life. I AM the power of God to HAVE.

I am the fiery strength of God, the living force of vitality that goes forth with divine intention and authority. My creativity is Love in action, and everything I do is victorious. My divine power is the thought that I WILL, and every door swings open before that power.

I have divine aspirations to fulfill my highest destiny, and with enthusiasm I move forward, forever illuminated by the higher vision. I see that which is mine to do, and I do it with ease, devotion, and gladness, and I am blessed with the treasures of heaven, for that is what I SEE.

I walk in the footsteps of my Self, and my path is sure. My ideals have been formulated in the crucible of my mind and are forged in divine design in my heart. In joyful freedom I now follow my heart, for I have seen my destiny, and what I see, I KNOW. [5]

On what level is God meeting you now? Above the quicksand of worry and the briar patch of anxiety, watch with awe and wonder as your life shifts dramatically to reveal the work, will, and way of Spirit.

The basic theme of my book, *Living a Life of Joy,* is: "There is no sense worrying about anything, everything's just fine." I go on to say . . .

> That's not ostrich or Pollyanna thinking—it's a strategic debil-itating strike aimed right at the heart of the ego who loves woe and has elevated the word *victim* to celebrity status. This shift in think-ing and feeling will put us into alignment with our true nature where all is perfect right now. We don't say it's going to be okay. That's pointing to the future, denying the reality inherent in the present moment and indicating that matter and minds have to be manipulated in order for the situation to change.
>
> What happens to us when we stop fretting and, regardless of appearances, turn our minds to the positive side of life? We loosen up, get lighter, the ego is weakened, and the power from within that reveals the all good begins to flow. We may even take time to play a little and let the responsibility for the "serious" part of our lives be handled by a higher wisdom and intelligence. That's when miracles seem to be multiplied daily.[6]

Another way to move above the currents of worry is to contem-plate three particular aspects of your being: Love, Harmony, and Peace. The key here is to become polarized in the highest vibration of each pole. Remember that love and hate, harmony and hostility, and peace and violence are all poles of the same thing with many degrees between them. What we want to do is to raise our mental vibrations so that we polarize in the highest extreme of each pole and thus be invulnerable to the planes of manifestation below.

Draw a triangle with Love at the top point, Harmony at the lower left point, and Peace at the base on the right. See the poles of polari-ty in the form of this triangle, and with purpose of mind and with the feeling nature activated, move up to the highest degree of Love, Harmony, and Peace. Lock into those energies in consciousness, then place yourself right in the middle of the triangle. Stay there and radiate the energies as a great searchlight. You will do more for your-self and others with this exercise than you can imagine.

> *Let Love flow forth from every heart.*
> *Let Harmony reign in every soul.*
> *Let Peace be the common bond.*

We used the triangle exercise in a 1999 workshop, and one of the participants wrote us later:

"The sacred Triangle of Love, Harmony, and Peace worked mir-acles on the journey home. It worked on five crying babies all around us and even on the food we were served. Then when we were in St. Louis, flight after flight was cancelled into our area due to heavy thunderstorms. So we constructed that Sacred Triangle over the country to Michigan and our flight left on time. Oh, here's another story. A friend and I later drove to Virginia, and before we left to come home we put the triangle around us and the car. In Ohio, I sud-denly had an urge to stop for lunch (no plans to do this; it was previ-ously agreed we would stop only to get gas). We stopped, a bad storm blew in, but we were safe. We later found out there were tornado warnings and 'touch-downs' in the county where we would have been if we hadn't stopped."

Look again now at the mythological picture. It is a woman in bed, face tightened in an expression of fear, hand on brow, as the roof (ceiling) is caving in. The key words are: *"If anything can go wrong, it will."* In interpreting this, we see that she is in a bedroom, which is a symbol of privacy, and the bed signifies a need for rest. The point is: The worry and anxiety have placed her in isolation (her choice), away from the activities of life and the verbalization of others. The ceiling falling in symbolizes self-punishment for perceived guilt—guilt for expecting the worst in life, which she knows is a denial of God. The expression of fear is her consciousness of unfulfilled desires, some of which she considers "forbidden." And the hand on the brow is a nonverbal statement of "woe is me."

But now we see that her eyes are closed, her head turned to the side on the pillow. She is asleep! In her dream, she is playing out a self-scripted scenario of her feelings about life. The anxiety disorders are all a dream and not a reality. It is an ego-dream. And how does she—representing all who live with constant worry—awaken from the dream and remove the mask? Exactly what we've been doing in this chapter—building our faith in that which is real. As we work positively with the planetary energies; free the inner archetypes; expose our fears to the light; move into the higher frequencies in consciousness; break the ego-connection by understanding and knowing there's really nothing to worry about; and polarize in the highest aspects of Love, Harmony, and Peace, our faith power begins to shine as bright as the noonday sun—and the clouds of worry and anxiety are quickly scattered. We become the faith of God in action . . . and the mask of the Worrier is removed.

chapter
eight

THE YIELDER

Neville Chamberlain, British prime minister from 1937 to 1940, was famous for his policy of appeasement toward Nazi Germany and his declaration of "peace for our time." He *yielded* to Hitler, and in the Munich Agreement of 1938, Germany was given part of Czechoslovakia, one of the tragic blunders that led to World War II.

The Chamberlain mind-set of truckle and kowtow is a part of the collective consciousness, and men and women today continue to practice this approval-seeking at any price—usually to the detriment of all concerned. I know that I compromised my spiritual integrity in the business world when I yielded to certain clients' outrageous demands. "It's his money," I may have thought, or "I'll do what I have to do to keep the account."

As I matured in my perspectives on life, I finally reached the point where I'd had it with a go-along-for-harmony's-sake attitude and began to show some backbone. But the Yielder mask was put back on when our daughters were teenagers. Jan and I wanted their friends to think we were cool, and we frequently looked the other way to avoid any kind of unpleasantness in the family environment. That was dumb. It was like the Munich Agreement, and things got so out of control that our home almost became a battle zone. Fortunately, that mask was finally peeled off and order was restored—at least to a

85

level that offered some semblance of calm cooperation.

As with other masks, there are degrees of Yielders. Some go along to get along, while others find themselves in desperate interpersonal relationships. We'll look at the low-impact situations first, but even those can serve as an obstacle to health, wealth, and success. I call it the echo syndrome. People will say things such as: "The flu bug is going around," "This good economy can't last," or "Don't expect too much in life or you'll be disappointed." And the Yielder, who may not feel this way at all, will play back the same tune—just to be agreeable, nice, or ingratiating. This sets up a negative vibration in consciousness that can attract adverse situations of a like manner. To not say anything is placid agreement, so why not speak out and say what you believe? "I'm not concerned about sickness," "Prosperity is based on consciousness and not the stock market," or "I expect only good things to happen in my life." (If that's not what you believe, you'd better work on your belief system.)

It also seems as though the Yielder is vulnerable to being taken advantage of by relatives and "friends" who are thinking only about their own personal agendas and know that Mr. or Mrs. Soft-Touch will be submissive and servile. After all, the Yielders want *everyone* to love and appreciate them—that's all that counts—so they naturally attract freeloaders, unannounced visitors, and unusual requests that would be considered highly inconsiderate to one without such a mask. The Yielders simply do not know how to say no.

Now we come to those very serious situations where the one wearing the Yielder mask could be considered neurotic or compulsive. The following story was told to me by a friend of a woman named Norma. Within months after Norma married Gerard, he began to physically abuse her—and each time, they would make up and go on as though nothing had happened. Of course, it only got worse. Shortly after their first anniversary, he pushed her down the stairs and broke her arm. "It was an accident," she told her friends. Gerard apologized with flowing tears, and promised he would never hurt her again. The battering increased, and Norma kept taking Gerard back

As we totally are:

Loving + loved

Joyous

Peaceful

Abundant

Totally fulfilled
superbeings created by God
to continue the creative
process from heaven to earth.

Don't let this day fly away.

HOTEL SANTA FE
THE HACIENDA AND SPA

~~Desk/Papers~~

QB?

~~Books.~~

Clothes

~~Dark wash~~

This week

D/W

· I have
plenty ·

not enough

Fear

Love
Abundant
~~Has~~ $

Bank

Water, More

Walk or Zumba

phel cheemia kóchii
Happy New Year

(505) 982-1200 • (800) 825-9876 • Fax (505) 984-2211
stay@hotelsantafe.com • www.hotelsantafe.com

until he nearly choked her to death. She called the police and had him arrested—but the Yielder mask was so entrenched that she visited him in jail and later dropped the charges. She says he's a changed man and wants their life to continue together. To the Yielder, suffering is a part of life that must be endured, regardless of the consequences.

I recognized a similar type of Yielder in an acquaintance several years ago. She always looked the other way and refused to say anything to her husband about his affairs with other women. To her, the marriage was more important than fidelity, but she paid the price with chronic physical problems, primarily in the throat. It wasn't until later, when I read Louise Hay's fine book, *You Can Heal Your Life*, that I saw the parallel. Louise wrote:

> The throat represents our ability to "speak up" for ourselves, to "ask for what we want," to say "I am," etc. When we have throat problems, it usually means that we do not feel we have the right to do these things. We feel inadequate to stand up for ourselves.
>
> The throat also represents the creative flow in the body. This is where we express our creativity; and when our creativity is stifled and frustrated, we often have throat problems. We all know many people who live their whole lives for others. They never once get to do what they want to do. They are always pleasing mothers/fathers/spouses/lovers/bosses. Tonsillitis and thyroid problems are just frustrated creativity resulting from not being able to do what you want to do.[1]

Since listing the masks that bind us in our *Quartus Reports*, I have received only three letters relating to the Yielder. A woman in Australia wrote: "The problems I have are mostly emotional—the damage done over a lifetime—unwanted, unloving family, lousy marriage, and so on. And the mask that fits best for me is Yielder because I always had to give or give in."

From a man in New York: "I've been a big-time Yielder because that was what I was taught as a child—that rewards came from pleasing my parents, and punishment came if I didn't. Same thing with teachers, friends, and bosses. I wanted to be liked and accepted, and I realize now that this desire for approval, which is considered normal in society, was way beyond the norm. My need for love and attention became obsessive, which was particularly true with my ex-wife. In my relationship with her, I think it was karmic payback. I probably wore the Tyrant mask in a past life and was trying to make amends in this one."

And a man in Texas said: "The roles of husband and wife were reversed in our home for many years. I wore the apron, cooked the meals, and tended to the house—not because I particularly wanted to, but because I thought it would please her. I was determined to make the marriage work, but when it became obvious that *nothing* I did pleased her, I gave up on the marriage."

The psychological profile of the Yielder shows a neurotic need for affection, with an indiscriminate desire to please everyone. The point of balance is not found in oneself, but in others—with their approval being the only thing that counts. Yielders are fearful of self-assertion, and will do everything possible to avoid conflict, including voicing their own opinions on matters of importance. Also, there is an almost desperate dependence on others for personal happiness.

This usually begins with parents who judge children by adult standards—mothers and fathers who recognize failure rather than accomplishment—which, to children, results in a response that they're not good enough. This causes kids to accept helplessness, which in turn forces them to try to win the affection of others. By being totally accommodating, they feel that they will be more accepted.

With this form of emotional bent, children grow up completely vulnerable to the planetary energies, with peace at any price being the overriding attitude. There will be strong identification with the mother—even though she may be responsible for the problem—and the kids will either cling to their parents' home, or move back home during the early adult years. As time goes on, there will be a tendency to want to sacrifice themselves for others. There will also be an inclination to waste and scatter their forces. They will play the let-me-please-you role rather than be themselves, and may be considered "plastic" personalities—very moldable to others' feelings. Love is used in manipulative ways for personal gain, and these individuals may be excessively complimentary—with a tendency to fawn over people to gain approval.

When the archetypes are repressed, these individuals will look longingly to the past for joys once felt—yet the images of the future are fearful. There is great insecurity and a defeatist attitude—a belief in sacrifice and suffering, which can only be alleviated by others. The mythological picture of the Yielder is a woman on her knees looking up at a man, her arms stretched toward him. The key words are: *"One who will do anything to please another."* Write what you see in your journal.

Removing the Mask

Lesson 14 in *The Jesus Code* says in part: *No person, place, thing, condition, or situation in the external world has power over you or to create anew for you. Place your undivided dependence on Spirit within, and Love will meet your needs.*[2]

Yes! No one has power over you unless you give it to them, which then makes them the ruler. The only power on earth is within you, so begin now to withdraw your projections of subservience on others. The Spirit within you is your power and authority. But even engaging in the simple act of trying to *get* something from another person— playing the Yielder in order to have him or her fulfill a particular need—means removing yourself from the loving, omnipresent activity of God. Affirm with mind and heart right now that no person in this world has power over you! Take responsibility for your life, and call on your spiritual strength and will to lift you out of a sense of dependence on others.

Think on these thoughts:

> *I am able to think for myself and make my own decisions.*
> *I speak up for myself.*
> *I do not depend on others for my happiness.*
> *I do not have to please everyone.*
> *I am Self-sufficient.*
> *I do what I want to do.*
> *I approve of the individual I am.*
> *I am strong.*
> *I am responsible.*
> *I am worthy.*

In Suzanne Harrill's book, *Affirm Your Self*, she offers these affirmative exercises on worthiness and unconditional love, both of which are vital in removing the Yielder mask.

Worthiness

> *I cannot earn being worthy of love and acceptance.*
> *It is my birthright.*
> *Nothing I do, say, or think can change this truth.*
> *I am a unique expression of the Higher Power.*
> *I am worthy and of value regardless of whether I have accepted this or not.*
> *Today, I choose to believe I am of value and am an important part of life.*
> *I am worthy because I exist.*[3]

Unconditional Love

I no longer expect anyone else to love me unconditionally.

If I turn my power over to others by relying on them for my good feelings, then I am bounced around by their moods and their ability to love.

When I turn within and connect with my inner Self, a direct link to the Higher Power, I learn to love myself.

Today, when I feel lonely, unworthy, separate from others, and in need of love, I will turn inward and ask my inner Self for this love without conditions.

I remember the truth that I cannot earn love, as it is already available as my birthright.

I unconditionally love myself.[4]

The Yielder must also understand what he or she is projecting on others. If you are a Yielder, consider the thoughts and feelings that you have repressed—then realize that this energy must be expressed, and repressed energy is expressed through projection. For example, if you feel that your husband, wife, father, or mother does not give you the love that you desperately desire, have you considered that maybe *your* love vibration is weak—that you truly do not feel love for yourself or others? The other person picks this up and plays it out for you. Remember that everyone in your life is there through the law of attraction, and whether you consider them good, bad, or indifferent, they are there to help you experience your self.

In *A Spiritual Philosophy for the New World*, I wrote:

> Everyone in your personal world will give you the opportunity to experience yourself through projection, which can work in two ways: (1) Someone to whom you are attracted may reject you based on a radiation of distorted ego energy from the unconscious level of your mind, which either turns them off or enables them to play out your unconscious feeling for you. This rejection is a signal that you are being sabotaged by something within *you*, having

nothing at all to do with the other person. And (2) someone can act as a mirror for you, enabling you to consciously see, sometimes in great detail, exactly what ego characteristics you are projecting. Remember, it is never "out there"—it is always within.[5]

Sondra Ray, creator of the Loving Relationships Training, states a metaphysical law:

> *People treat you the way you treat yourself.* Jesus said, "Love thy neighbor as *thyself*." One definition of love is ultimate self-approval. If you love yourself, you will automatically give others the opportunity to love you. If you hate yourself, you will not allow others to love you. If your self-esteem is low and someone loves and accepts you, you will reject them, try to change them, or think they are lying. When you blame the world for lacking love, you are creating still more negative mental mass, which makes things worse for you.[6]

Sondra also says:

> A *personal law* is your most negative thought about yourself. Let's imagine that yours is "I never get what I really want." Upon this you would therefore have built many negative beliefs. The worst part about your personal law is that you are unconsciously putting out a command to the universe telepathically whether you speak or not. In the case above, you would be putting out: "People! Don't give me what I want!" Others would have to respond to you appropriately. If you didn't know you had this personal law (most people don't), then you might wonder why others get what they want and you don't.[7]

Work with this meditation to shift consciousness above the projection level.

God is infinite Love, the great Identity in all relationships, the eternal essence of all forms, and this Absolute All-That-Is, is my very divine consciousness.

I lift up my mind and heart to be aware, to understand, and to know that the divine Presence I AM is the source, cause, and quality of every relationship in my life.

I am conscious of the inner Presence as my loving experience of fulfillment, as the harmony in every connection with another being. I am conscious of the constant activity of this mind of total goodwill and joyful unity; therefore, my consciousness is filled with the Love of right relations.

Through my consciousness of my God-Self as my source of companionship, friendship, and the quality of every love experience, I draw into my mind and feeling nature the Light of Spirit. This Light is the essence of every bonding with another; thus, my consciousness of the Master Self I AM is the cause of every good and perfect relationship.

My inner Light draws to me now those with whom I can relate in love, peace, and joy. Because it is the principle of right relations in action, my desires are beautifully fulfilled; my needs are easily met.

The divine consciousness I AM is forever securing the bond of harmlessness and harmony between me and everyone else in my world. Therefore, I am totally confident to let God appear as each and every relationship in my life.

When I am aware of my divine consciousness as my total fulfillment, I am totally fulfilled. I am now aware of this truth, and I relax in the knowledge that the activity of divine attraction and right relations is eternally operating in my life. I simply have to be aware of the flow of the creative energy that is continuously radiating from within. I am now aware. I am now in the flow.

Look at the mythological picture once more—the woman on her knees looking up at a man, her arms stretched toward him. The key words are: *"One who will do anything to please another."* What you may not have seen in your imagination was that the man was reaching down with his hands to meet hers. And notice the loving expression on his face. She was striving to *get* love from another when she had it all the time. All she needed was to *accept* herself as a spiritual being who has been given everything—to *know* her strength, power, and worthiness—and *rise up* into the embrace of unconditional love.

There is an interesting facet in the Yielder mask. When one simply becomes aware that he or she is wearing such a disguise, something clicks in consciousness, and a greater sense of confidence begins to dawn. "I can be myself," one might say, "not the fawning, plastic self I thought I was, but a courageous, resourceful, self-sufficient soul on equal footing with everyone. I can now be who I am in truth with poise and dignity."

The mask is gone. Congratulations.

chapter
nine

THE MEDDLER

Meddler: "One who interferes without being asked . . . to tamper deviously in the affairs of others . . . a busybody" (Webster's). We have all known Meddlers, and this particular mask seems to have some of the elements of three other masks—the Manipulator, the Tyrant, and the Opinionated, with a touch of the Fanatic added for good measure. These men and women just won't mind their own business. They pry with a scheme, display a know-it-all attitude, and push with a zeal that is oppressive to say the least. And the excuse is usually, "I just want to help."

Psychologically, the Meddler is one who seeks to live through others—the former also-ran beauty queen who insists that her daughter become Miss America, the college football player who didn't fulfill his dreams envisions his son being drafted by the NFL, the mother and father who try to realize their hopes, wishes, and dreams through their offspring. They view the desires and ideals of their children as completely different from those of the family as a whole, and strive to cast lives in the mold of the parental image with an insistence on conformity. If we trace this behavior and attitude back to the meddler's childhood, we see indifference on the part of the parents, disparaging remarks, a lack of warmth, unkept promises, and little respect for the child's emotional needs—all of this while practicing what may be called "indirect domination." To compensate, the individual will grow up with the attitude, perhaps unconscious, to right the injustice he or she may have felt—and at any cost.

Fay was a classic Meddler, and her son, Bob, remembers her well. "My father died when I was six, and from then on, everything in my life had to be totally organized. Free time to just play with my friends was a no-no. I had to be exposed to the finer things of life, like music and ballroom dancing. I wanted to play football, but Mother convinced the coach that I was too small and would get hurt. The girls I dated had to be approved by her, otherwise I couldn't use the family car, and when I married Sally against Mother's will (Sally was a Catholic), I was cut off completely—I didn't realize to what extent until Mother died."

The Meddler seems to have an indiscriminate need to take advantage of others and get the better of them—to make them captives for exploitation, leading to distorted personalities. A woman I'll call Ruth refused to let her children have friends in their home for fear that they would "contaminate" her beloved ones. This, of course, ruled out any extracurricular activities at school, and her kids became maladjusted loners.

Jan and I also remember a friend who took complete control of his son's life and began training him to be a football hero someday—and the son hated every minute of it. The man sold insurance and was able to maintain flexible hours, which meant that every day after school and on the weekends, they would practice, practice, practice. Harsh words were the norm when the child dropped a pass. By the time the youngster reached high school, he was so bent out of shape mentally that his grades suffered and he had few friends. Fortunately, he finally rebelled and told his father that sports were not for him, that he wanted to play in the band. Music offered him the recovery he needed, but the father "washed his hands" of the son and soon asked the wife for a divorce. A Meddler's world had fallen apart.

Not all Meddlers are parents, though. A woman at a workshop

said that when she was dating her boyfriend, she began to notice strange things. He started getting extremely possessive, stopping by her workplace at the oddest times "to check up on her," and once she caught him following her from the office to the grocery store after work. When they did get together, she was thoroughly questioned about anyone she had talked to during the day. He also called her at work incessantly with the idea of getting her fired for bringing her personal life to the office, and she found out later that he was trying to arrange a job for her at his own place of employment.

With the Meddler personality, the planetary energies can also emphasize smothering/mothering tendencies in both men and women. The father will find it difficult to grant his children independence; the mother will want to shield the offspring from the outer world. There is a dominant desire for power over others, and as strange as this may seem, the power is often used to gain *fame* for the Meddler. They wish to mold others, live through the person they have "created"—yet with an element of distrust always present. They are critical, analytical, selfish, intolerant of others' views, and usually food fanatics. They show righteous indignation and little patience, and are addicted to malicious talk.

As the inner archetypes are repressed, the individual's attitude and behavior worsens. The Meddler will not be concerned about the rights of others, and will be unable to adopt new ideas, refusing to listen to anyone else's advice. Meddlers are continually suspicious of the motives of others, are constantly frustrated, and possess a morbid curiosity.

The mythological picture is either a man or woman standing in front of the opposite sex and holding out a bouquet of flowers. The other hand, behind the back, is holding a sword. The key words are: *"Trust me. I only want what's best for you."* Look at the symbols and describe the picture in your journal.

Those who interfere in the lives of others suffer from self-centeredness, self-importance, selfish personal ambition, and devious manipulation. They are the active schemers in the world today, unable to work with faith and love. The forces of such a personality are seated in the sacral center.

In *Anatomy of the Spirit*, Caroline Myss writes: "This chakra resonates to our need for relationships with other people and our need to control to some extent the dynamics of our physical environment. All attachments by which we maintain control over our external lives, such as authority, other people, or money, are linked through this chakra to our energy field and physical body."[1]

Myss also says that one of the primary fears associated with this chakra is the fear of losing control. If we have no control over others, it is difficult to meddle in their lives. Later, as we remove this mask, we'll work with the sacral chakra. But first, I feel it is important for you to learn how to escape from the Meddler's energy. Your very life may depend on it.

If you recognize a Meddler in your space and feel that you are succumbing to his or her machinations, ask yourself if you are a Victim, a Yielder, or both. Then go back and read the "Removing the Mask" sections in both chapters. Don't fall for the line "I just want to help" or "I only want what's best for you." Do what is necessary right now to get out from under this potentially dangerous energy. It may seem harmless and benign at first, but it can wreak havoc in your life if you let yourself be monopolized by such a person.

For example, Doris got a general power of attorney, cleaned out her mother's bank account, and forced her into a nursing home. And Abby kept looking for the "good" in Paul, even when he isolated her from family and friends, forged her name on several checks, and eventually resorted to physically abusing her. She was afraid she would lose him if she accused him or made him angry. Don't take chances. No one is more important than *you*, so take control of your life now!

Bring the image into your mind of someone you consider to be meddling in your life. Remember that this mask may not be as apparent as the others, so if you're not sure, ask yourself these questions: From whom am I always seeking approval? With whom do I assume a role, feeling that I cannot really be myself? Who is imposing their rules on me? With whom do I feel oppressive energy? Who makes me feel emotionally insecure and mentally weak? Who am I afraid of? Who makes me feel that I will never be good enough? Who is the most critical person in my life? Who focuses on my weaknesses rather than my strengths? With whom do I hide my true feelings?

Now see a psychic cord between your energy field and that of this person. It is an emotional and mental attachment that is draining away your freedom; and screening out your creative success, prosperity, well-being, and happiness. Meddlers can mess with your mind and emotions and also affect your physical-material world. So with purpose of mind, cut that cord! Use a sharp knife and see it slicing through the cord—then pull out the roots from the place where you feel the cord was attached to you physically. Energy follows thought, so this is more than just an imaginary exercise. It works!

If you feel almost smothered with a Meddler's energy, think of it as an octopus with its eight arms covered with suckers all around you and literally squeezing you. Take the knife again, and in your imagination, begin to free yourself by cutting off the arms one by one. Then sever the head, and watch as the creature slowly dissolves before your eyes. You may also find a picture of the one you feel is an oppressive Meddler, plan a special releasing ceremony, and burn the picture. This may seem extreme, but we have found that the Meddler can be one of the most treacherous masks because it is so covert, and the motives of the wearer so veiled. The Manipulator, Tyrant, Opinionated, and Fanatic masks are much easier to spot, but the Meddler works in the shadows and is slippery, subtle, and sneaky. Keep in mind that the releasing exercises discussed here will not harm the Meddler in any way. He or she will, unconsciously, feel a protective shield around you, or will no longer be interested in controlling you or interfering in your life. Another target will be selected.

Now think on these thoughts:

> *I am free of domination from others.*
> *Someone else's thoughts and opinions cannot take*
> *away my power.*
> *I can be myself without concern for what anyone thinks.*
> *I approve, appreciate, and love myself.*
> *I no longer seek anyone else's approval.*
> *I am my own person.*
> *I recognize my true worth.*
> *I am strong mentally and secure emotionally.*

And continue with . . .

> *I AM a radiating center of total peace.*
> *I AM the harmony that will never cease.*
> *I AM the power to do, to have, and to be.*
> *I AM the life that is eternally free.*
> *I AM the way, the truth, and the light.*
> *I AM an eagle in preparation for flight.*

Now let's look at the other side of the coin. If *you* are the Meddler, the very fact that you are reading this book tells me that you haven't moved into the extremist position. There's still hope because of the spiritual vibration you feel in consciousness. You want to do the right thing, but events and circumstances have led you on the path of interference in the lives of others . . . but it's not too late to turn back.

Removing the Mask

The first thing to do is to make a commitment to *mind your own business*. And what is your business? It is to concentrate on your own spiritual awakening and find your delight there, rather than trying to live someone else's life. Your daughter, son, mother, father, sister, brother, or friend all deserve the right to be the captains of their own ship, masters of their own destiny. You don't know what's best for them, and you certainly don't have the authority to take away the opportunity for the other person to grow physically, emotionally, mentally, and spiritually. Each one of us came in with our piece of the divine puzzle, a particular plan to implement, and to interfere with that purpose will call for a karmic payback of utmost severity.

In *The Angels Within Us*, I wrote:

> More karmic effects result from relationships than from any other activity of life. Every thought, word, and action in one way or another affects a relationship, for "the measure you give will be the measure you get" (Matthew 7:2). . . . The injunction to "love one another" and follow the Golden Rule is truly a guide to living more harmoniously through the right application of karmic law. By being consciously aware that we always reap what we sow, we can begin to build right relations—with loving thoughts, encouraging words, and constructive action—from the home to the workplace, and everywhere in between.[2]

If you really want to help others, love them unconditionally—with no strings attached—and understand that the only allegiance they owe you is by right of consciousness. You are either attracting or repelling. Instead of living through others, live as and through the person you are, an individual being here on earth for a period of time to understand and know God, life, and the meaning of this world. Realize your own hopes, wishes, and dreams by seeing the ideal life for *you*; holding it firm in consciousness; thinking thoughts of truth; speaking words of power; and letting Spirit work through you, as you.

This perfect world for you—your ideal life—never includes taking advantage of others, being possessive or jealous, or infringing on the rights of others regardless of how much you "love" them. As Kahlil Gibran put it, *"Let there be spaces in your togetherness, and let the winds of the heavens dance between you."*

Earlier we referred to the sacral chakra. According to Ageless Wisdom texts, it is the seat of anger, malice, and hatred, astrologically shown as Mars in Scorpio. This particular alignment, according to metaphysical astrologer Isabel M. Hickey, is "fixed fire in a water sign (which) generates steam. Intense, proud, strong-willed, stubborn where convictions are concerned. Here the animal must be tamed for the personality must be redeemed. . . . Must learn to draw to him through love, not fear. . . . Self-discipline is a necessity."[3] Does this describe you?

Caroline Myss says:

> The sacred truth inherent in the second chakra is *Honor One Another*. This truth applies to our interactions with each other and with all forms of life. . . . The spiritual challenge of the second chakra is to learn to interact consciously with others: to form unions with people who support our development and to release relationships that handicap our growth. . . . The challenge of the second chakra is to learn what motivates us to make the choices we do. In learning about our motivations, we learn about the content of our spirits. Are you filled with fear, or are you filled with faith? Every choice we make contains the energy of either faith or fear, and the outcome of every decision reflects to some extent that faith or fear. This dynamic of choice guarantees that we cannot run away from ourselves or our decisions.[4]

Focus on this energy center below the navel. Take several deep breaths and exhale slowly, and as you do, feel the sacral center beginning to radiate as a searchlight shining in all directions. Now contemplate these words, drawing forth the energy behind them: *uprightness . . . nobility . . . respect . . . reverence . . . honor.* Keep working until you feel a definite shift taking place in consciousness, feeling yourself as an upright and noble person. Then let the sweep of your consciousness take in your entire family, your friends, and anyone else you have thought worthy of your meddling, and bathe them with your new perspective of seeing them with respect, reverence, and honor. Release everyone to their highest good. Now see the light of the sacral center begin to rise, moving upward, anchoring in the throat center and radiating out as creative power. In this energy stream, see your ideal life in all its aspects. The objective is to see a whole new world with you at the center, a life that doesn't include relying on someone else for your happiness and fulfillment. See optimal creative success, abundant prosperity, a whole and well physical body, and loving relationships.

The Wisdom Teachings tell us that there must be a relationship between the sacral and throat chakras. "This relation, when lacking, produces friction. There will be no real expression of 'the true' until the forces of the creative center below the diaphragm are raised to the creative center of the throat. Then 'the Word . . . will be made flesh' and a true expression of the soul upon the physical plane will be seen."[5]

Work with this meditation and see the Word made flesh, the unity of Spirit and matter:

> *I now give to my world all that was perceived to be missing. I see the radiant energies going before me to fill every cup and make all things new.*
>
> *I see myself with a magnificently healthy body in perfect order, where every cell is in the image of the perfect pattern, and I am whole and complete.*
>
> *A beautiful harvest of abundance is springing forth at every moment, ready for gathering. I am the Spirit of Infinite Plenty, the Shining Sun of Supply.*
>
> *The creative activity of God is flowing through me now, and my mind is responsive to divine thoughts of success.*
>
> *My inner Light now draws to me those with whom I can relate to in love, peace, and joy. The activity of right relations is eternally operating in my life.*
>
> *There is wholeness, abundance, success, and ideal relationships. I see myself living as I have always dreamed, yet now the dream is a reality, for I have awakened to the vision of truth.*

Think again about the mythological picture—the man or woman standing in front of the opposite sex and holding a bouquet of flowers. The other hand, behind the back, is holding a sword. The key words are: *"Trust me. I only want what's best for you."* The Meddler is two-faced, offering love and friendship (flowers), but with an ulterior motive (the sword). The Meddler wants to intrude in the other person's life to satisfy his or her emptiness in life, or to carry out a personal agenda. The Meddler gains entrance into another's consciousness simply by being a family member, a friend, or loved one— and once in, they begin to exercise their craftiness. If the flowers are being offered to you, and your intuitive nature tells you not to be pulled in, listen! Refuse to come under the domination (subtle or not) of others. Stand tall and strong with the courage of your convictions, and treat the person as you would someone wearing the Manipulator, Tyrant, or Opinionated mask: with divine detachment, forgiveness, unconditional love, harmlessness, and spiritual understanding.

If you are the one offering the flowers and you see yourself as a Meddler, drop the sword *and* the flowers. Make the choice now to renounce possessive love; make the decision to do unto others as you would have them do unto you. Show only kindness, compassion, and unconditional love toward others, and realize that the only person in the world that you have to deal with is yourself. Release everyone to follow their own path, and with a new self-discipline, follow your own. Later, you may speak the words of Gibran to your former prey:

> *We are friends.*
> *I want nothing from you, and you want nothing from me.*
> *We share life.*

That's when you know the mask has been completely removed.

chapter
ten

THE PRIDEFUL

The Prideful mask can take many forms. First, there is the personality that believes *it* is the higher power, that God is an outside force, and the reliance must be placed on human nature for survival. Such individuals will follow only the desires of the ego and are seen as haughty and pretentious, with much self-praise. There is also the ego mask of pride that is worn to disguise low self-worth, where these individuals will play a role in an attempt to show others that they are more than they appear to be. This is a masking of fears, usually through arrogance. We've all known people who were vain and pompous on the outside, but were tied in knots on the inside—the outer bravado trying to hide the inner apprehension and vulnerabilities.

A former neighbor certainly fits the latter description. He enjoyed playing the part of a pompous braggart, always talking (among the men) of his sexual exploits with younger women (he was married at the time), his success in business, and the money he made as a salesman. As I got to know him better, the mask became so transparent that I could clearly see his inner turmoil. He was a frightened man, afraid of possible downturns in the economy, of growing older, and of not being able to compete with the "young Turks" in the company where he worked. He was an ego-dominated individual, and the last we heard, most of what he had feared he had attracted.

*Pride, like the magnet, constantly points to one
object, self; but unlike the magnet, it has no attractive pole,
but at all points repels.*
— Colton

The Prideful mask can also come from an overzealous, competitive attitude to "prove something." Ed looked at the list of masks that I introduced in *The Quartus Report* before starting on this book, and selected the Prideful as one he has worn.

He wrote: "I grew up in a family with a near-poverty environment, and my brothers and I were always competing with each other for everything—including food, clothing, and attention from our parents. (As a side note, I always ate faster than the others so I could have a second helping, and I embarrassed my wife after we were married with my table manners.) Also, I was big for my age, so I learned to intimidate at an early age and had a lot of fights with kids at school to prove 'who was the best.' And until a few years ago, I guess I'd been doing that for most of my life, trying to 'show up' everyone. The Prideful mask was on pretty tight, and it took a business failure, the loss of what friends I had left, and a separation from my wife to wake me up. During all this, I found God and humility, and I turned my life around. Now I have self-respect . . . wish I had found it sooner."

The parental environment is a major influence, as we see in Tracey's glimpse into her Prideful days. She wrote: "I grew up in a family that was considered an 'old family' in the community, sort of the rock of the town—big house from Grandpa, all the trimmings of social 'class.' Even though my parents squandered all the money and we were living on image alone, I still played the part, which wasn't difficult because I was told from childhood that we were better than others. I believed it—and acted the part to perfection. But when I married, my husband wasn't into snobbery, didn't give a bleep about family tradition, and told me to give up the airs or get out. Sometimes it's hard to break old patterns, but I stayed and changed, and I even planted a garden to get more 'earthy.'"

I've worn the Prideful mask, too. In the late 1960s, I was vice president of a highly successful Houston advertising agency, and one day I had a telephone call. The voice on the line said that Bud Adams, owner of the Houston Oilers (now the Tennessee Titans) wanted to talk to me about forming my own ad agency. Something inside said, "Be discerning!" In other words, *watch your step*. I was too excited to listen, and met with him the next day.

During that meeting he offered to set me up with five million dollars in new accounts. There would be a few strings attached, and the inner voice kept insisting that I *think* before agreeing to anything. No, this was too good to even think about, so I agreed to the terms of the deal. Within 60 days, I found the talent I wanted for the key positions and opened the doors to a suite of plush offices.

Adams had come up with an idea for a product—a beverage called Quickick—that would compete with Gatorade, and with that base account, other blue-chippers soon came into the fold. The media said we were the largest start-from-scratch agency in Texas history. I was proud. Next, I traveled around the country making speeches at "kick-off parties" in NFL cities, meeting and shaking hands with the top professional football players of the day. (They would be my support group in promoting Quickick.) My self-importance was bursting at the seams. Then after our national advertising campaign was launched, we won the Grand Prix Award for the best consumer magazine advertising. I was *very* proud. Jan and I also traveled on the Oilers' plane for out-of-town games, and we were in high cotton. I was riding the peacock, and it felt good. But then something happened. Consumers didn't like the product that Adams spent millions of dollars to promote. It didn't taste good. The product was pulled off the market, and a multimillion dollar account went out the window. The easy ride turned bumpy, and other accounts waved good-bye. The Prideful mask was replaced with those resembling the Worrier, the Victim, and the Abandoned.

Earlier I mentioned *discernment*, which comes from a Latin term meaning "to know enough to keep separate." To be discerning means to be perceptive, astute, discriminating, and judicious. The inner voice had warned me in advance to keep separate from this supposed "deal of a lifetime"—but Adams touched my ego button, and once the offer was made, there was no turning back. Let's remember that when we refuse to listen to that voice of reason within, that heed for caution, we are following the dictates of ego to satisfy our personal needs. My desire was to be president of my own agency, which would have probably been realized if I had stayed where I was. But I chose instant gratification instead, and became consumed in pomp and swagger in the process.

Spiritual pride is also another repelling characteristic. One of the teachings in *The Jesus Code* is:

> Spiritual pride erects a wall in the one mind as a barrier to the light of wisdom and understanding. Darkness then prevails, and there is vulnerability to conflict and duplicity, for pride leads to arrogance and pretension. It is self-glorification in its lowest form. To fulfill the goal of life, serve with humility while steadfastly holding to Truth.[1]

I also point out in that chapter:

> To be spiritually proud is to be ego-centered, and the ego is the tempter. *Lead us not into temptation.* What temptation? Feelings of superiority, self-righteousness, and judgment. . . . Where before there was illumination, even if only a faint glow, now there is only the darkness of confusion. When darkness prevails, it can be compared to the dark night of the soul. And it all begins when we think of ourselves as knowing something that others don't, or having a power that others have not yet discovered, or because of our spiritual quest we judge ourselves as "good"—a little more righteous than our neighbor.[2]

He that is proud eats up himself; pride is his glass,
his trumpet, his chronicle, and whatever praises itself but
in the deed, devours the deed in the praise.
— Shakespeare

The planetary energies radiating on those who are prone to self-glorification will stimulate rash judgment, extravagance, and yes, sometimes a lack of discernment. The person may also be critical, irritable, and petty—and with that vibration in consciousness will attract the wrong type of friends and suffer legal entanglements. There is much hypocrisy and strong stubbornness, the desire for material success outweighing all other intentions. It is a "puffed up" ego (with corresponding problems with weight gain), with the individual wanting to dominate others. These people are usually arrogant and bombastic with a "me-first" attitude, and frequently have difficulties with their children.

When the inner archetypes are repressed, the person will begin to fear whatever is around the next corner, with an obsessive concern about the "evils" of this world. Emphasis will be placed on personal efforts rather than the power within as the way to achieve happiness. There is an unconscious fear of the "will of God"—with material living being more important than the spiritual way of life—the latter considered weak and ineffective.

Psychologically, we see compulsive traits from various other masks. The Prideful is a person who views life as dependent primarily on public acceptance, with a desperate need for social recognition. He or she craves power and has an inflated image of self (narcissism), with a fear of criticism or reproach. It begins with a lack of satisfying interactions with others in the first few years of life, either with the mother or father. As this leads to feelings of isolation, helplessness, and low self-worth, the child will develop unconscious patterns to compensate for what is perceived to be a lack of respect and the absence of admiration. The boy or girl (or man or woman) learns that anxieties can be relieved by being the center of attention—in the limelight—which fosters conceit and boastfulness, and the Prideful mask is donned.

Mythologically, we see a naked man riding a peacock. The key words are: *"One who thinks he is grander than others."* Study the symbols and write what you see in your journal, or make a sketch of how you view the picture.

Removing the Mask

I want to emphasize again how important it is to peel away this false face, because if we are riding the peacock, we are riding for a fall.

Pride goes before destruction, and a haughty spirit before a fall. (Prov.18:18)

When pride comes, then comes disgrace; but with the humble is wisdom. (Prov. 11:2.)

As John Ruskin, the famed English social reformer, stated, "Pride is at the bottom of all great mistakes. All the other passions do occasional good; but whenever pride puts in its word, everything goes wrong."

To remove this mask, let's do a bit of self-analysis. Open your journal to a new page, and contemplate the instructions and questions that follow. Write what comes to mind:

> Take a close look at yourself—as a field of consciousness, of mind and heart. Now, what do you feel you need for further progress in life?

> Look at what you value most in life and ask yourself why. Examine your priorities and see if they infringe on the rights of others.

How do you honestly feel about yourself? Is there clarity regarding your real thoughts and intentions?

Do you feel guilt stemming from any actions you have taken in the past? If yes, bring them to mind and forgive yourself, then take your perceived mistakes to the Light of Spirit to be dissolved.

How would you rate your one-on-one encounters with others? Do they represent love, peace, and joy? Why not?

Are you resistant to change? If yes, consider the reasons.

Are childhood behavior problems restricting you? Look closely at your level of maturity and decide what changes need to be made.

Why do you feel compelled to exaggerate your own importance? Remember that this is an exercise in self-analysis. Be honest.

Do you acquire possessions to show social status? Look closely at the symbols of materiality and ask yourself if you derive true pleasure from them.

Can you accept the fact that all limitations imposed upon you in life were self-imposed? Why do you think you limit yourself?

Can you express yourself without being overbearing and domineering? Why do you feel you have to prove something to others?

Why do you feel that you are not recognized for your true worth? Is it because, on some level of consciousness, you do not feel worthy?

Next, we should examine how we are being affected by the ego, which says that *it* is doing the work. We may see ourselves as a great success in business, or as a gifted writer, artist, teacher, healer—whatever. We think of ourselves as the wellspring of achievement, the begetter of wisdom, the fount of creativity, the source of enlightenment, the cause of cures. That's where pridefulness comes from—the belief that *we* are the doers, the healers, the movers and shakers in this world. But the truth is, we're not. We, as a personality, are the *channels* or *instruments* for Spirit. To think otherwise is nothing but ego-arrogance, which sets up a desperate need in us to seek approval from others, and we attract those who will confirm how "special" we are to reinforce the Prideful mask.

Vanity can work in two ways. I'm grand or I'm incomplete—both coming from ego. To me, the key here is to understand that *I of myself can do nothing . . . it is the Presence and Power within that does the work.* This way of thinking takes us away from pomposity *and* unfulfillment, grandiosity *and* debasement. It says that ego is not to be idolized or feared, which shifts our mind to Cause where we can assume our rightful function in the scheme of things—to simply be the consciousness through which Spirit works.

Let's contemplate this meditation, adapted from the chapter on "Materiality and Temptation" in *The Angels Within Us*:

> *I am the instrument through which the Master I AM expresses, and I place my dependence on this Holy One within rather than on anything in the outer world. I understand that the only responsibility that I have in life is to be conscious of my God-Self, and that that Self will then meet all of my responsibilities through me. I realize that as long as there is a human sense of being, I must not rely on that sense to free me from the illusions of this world. My reliance*

*must be totally on the Presence within, who is eternally radiating
the energy of all good into my world.*

*I now live as an open channel for you, my Lord and Master
Self, without spiritual pride, without relying on unrealized truth to
change my world, without distortions of reality. I will live in one-
ness with you as I walk the earth, enjoying every moment of my
journey and knowing that the Awakening will soon take place.[3]*

From here we see how important humility is. True humility
means being open and receptive to new ideas. It is being unpreten-
tious. It is the consciousness of consent, a willingness to be shown the
higher path through a surrender of the lower personality. With humility, our true worthiness begins to shine as bright as the noonday sun.

Yes, worthiness is a vital ingredient in removing the Prideful
mask, because one of the reasons we don that mask in the first place
is through a lack of self-approval. Think for a moment: Do you really approve of yourself? Do you like yourself enough to just be *you*?
Do you love yourself enough to put the vanity mask away? Louise
Hay has an exercise that will help:

> I have given this exercise to hundreds of people, and the results
> are phenomenal. For the next month, say over and over to yourself,
> "I APPROVE OF MYSELF."
>
> Do this three or four hundred times a day—at least. No, it's not
> too many times. When you are worrying, you go over your prob-
> lem at least that many times. Let "I approve of myself" become a
> walking mantra, something you just say over and over and over to
> yourself, almost nonstop.
>
> Saying "I approve of myself" is guaranteed to bring up every-
> thing buried in your consciousness that is in opposition. When the
> negative thoughts come up . . . this is the time to take mental con-
> trol. Give it no importance. Just see the thought for what it is,
> another way to keep you stuck in the past. Gently say to this
> thought, "I let you go, I approve of myself."[4]

Now let's look again at the mythological picture—a naked man riding a peacock. The key words are: *"One who thinks he is grander than others."* Nakedness is symbolic of shame and also a desire to flaunt as an exhibitionist. Put the two together, and we see one who is hiding what's on the inside by parading around—boasting, if you will—with blatant behavior. And the peacock, since ancient times, has been a symbol of pride. But look at the sadness in his face. There's no joy in self-glorification. He wants everyone to notice him, but those who do are only repelled.

If you've been riding the peacock, it's time to get off. You don't have to compensate with a Prideful mask, or play a role, or compete with anyone, or depend on anyone for your acceptance, or be the center of attention as a personality. The me-first attitude and the desire to dominate others is fading away. Your intention now is to live as an open channel for Spirit, knowing that the activity of God is the only power in your life—and you're giving the credit where credit is due. And you're beginning to approve of yourself—the marvelous being that you are in truth.

Relax now and just be yourself—and let the Prideful mask be removed.

chapter eleven

THE OBSESSED

The individual who is obsessed is one possessing compulsive ideas or irresistible urges—the overeater, the alcoholic, the gambler, the drug addict, the workaholic, the sexual fanatic—or one who has a fixation, an unnatural preoccupation, about some person or thing. Desires overwhelmingly out of control represent the true nature of this mask.

John Bradshaw, counselor and bestselling author, says:

> Neurotic shame is the root and fuel of all compulsive/addictive behaviors. My general working definition of compulsive/addictive behavior is "a pathological relationship to any mood-altering experience that has life-damaging consequences."
>
> The drivenness in any addiction is about the ruptured self, the belief that one is flawed as a person. The content of the addiction, whether it be an ingestive addiction or an activity addiction (like work, buying or gambling) is an attempt at an intimate relationship. The workaholic with his work, or the alcoholic with his booze, are having a love affair. Each one mood alters to avoid the feeling of loneliness and hurt in the underbelly of shame. Each addictive acting out creates life-damaging consequences which create more shame. The new shame fuels the cycle of addiction.
>
> The cycle begins with the false belief system that all addicts

have, that no one could want them or love them as they are. In fact, addicts can't love themselves. They are an object of scorn to themselves. This deep internalized shame gives rise to distorted thinking. The distorted thinking can be reduced to the belief that I'll be okay if I drink, eat, have sex, get more money, work harder, etc.[1]

A man I knew back in the '70s had a love affair—not only with whiskey, but with pills as well. Late one night, I had a call that he was going to commit suicide, and by the time I arrived at his apartment, he was passed out on the floor, having ingested a heavy combination of booze and tranquilizers. There was also a pistol on the coffee table, possibly to be used if all else failed. We got him to the emergency room on time, and later, on the advice of a psychiatrist, had him admitted to a mental health facility. With counseling, he finally straightened out his life. In retrospect, I can see that he was a lonely man (his wife had left him), and he certainly considered himself "flawed"—with little self-esteem. He was looking for something on the outside to make up for what was missing on the inside.

Men and women who are vulnerable to compulsive behavior, which usually stems from a jarring interpersonal experience in early life, will find the planetary energies impacting with great pressure. There will be much emotional suffering, frustration over a lack of achievement, and a blindness to the purpose of life. The person will lack stability and logic, have little social awareness, and will be solely concerned with the senses and the physical world. Yet there is a tendency to withdraw from the world. Because of the mental-emotional vibration of high impressionability, there is the risk of obsession by so-called guides or astral entities, providing a "doomsday voice in the head" that only adds to the turmoil within. The individual will also suffer from illusions and be easily influenced by people in physical form.

In intimate relationships, there is a feeling that love demands more sacrifice than the individual is willing to give. These are usually lonely, supersensitive people who try to evade responsibility, and there is definitely poor judgment where finances are concerned. If asked, they will be happy to tell you all about the skeletons in the family closet.

When the inner archetypes, the living energies, are repressed, primitive forces of the unconscious rise up to be overcome. The person will then live in an imaginary dream world with wild fantasies to escape reality. There is much inner struggle, an inability to learn from mistakes, and a tendency to be reckless and take impulsive action.

Now remember, as we've said about the other masks, there are degrees of compulsive behavior, and not everyone with an obsession will find the full range of these personality characteristics at work in consciousness. But find what applies to you, so that when we move to the healing process, you can remove the mask without difficulty.

Psychologically, the mask may be worn to compensate for guilt arising from perceived failure to live up to parents' expectations, memories of emotional wounds inflicted on the mother, sexual abuse from either parent, or dishonesty in adolescent years that is carried over into adulthood. It has been said that people with totally unwarranted feelings of guilt will repeatedly wash their hands. Guilt leads to deep-seated anxieties, with compulsive behavior used as a way to reduce the inner tension. The same thing may apply to people who are isolated from their peers through social judgment. And religious conversions later in life can bring a full range of "sins" to mind, which trigger guilt and the perceived need for punishment.

The mythological picture is a woman stuffing her mouth with something in both hands, fear on her face, body trembling. The key words are: *"One can only heal the inner by gratifying the outer."*

I have found that this symbolic portrait doesn't portray the full range of the obsessive personality because it focuses primarily on ingestive addiction, and as we've seen, there are many other forms it can take. A minister friend told me about his experience of being smothered by a member of his congregation. In his opinion, she was totally obsessed with him, having substituted him for her personal savior. She felt the minister would not only meet her spiritual needs, but she would also find her peace and happiness in him. In time, she became possessive, jealous, and totally intrusive in his life. One Sunday he gave a sermon—directed specifically at her—on how certain people become obsessed with others to meet their own needs. She got the point and backed off.

Amy said that when she and Floyd were going together, it was a fairly balanced and normal relationship, but when she tired of it and broke it off, he became a different man. "He actually *stalked* me—everywhere I went he was there, and he called and e-mailed me daily. He even wrote in the dust on my car, "You are mine!" I called the police, but they said they couldn't do anything. The problem was finally resolved when he lost his job and moved to another city."

A letter I received from Julia addresses another obsession. It was a rather lengthy letter, but I feel the major points are important for those who have an obsession with weight and food. She wrote:

"When I was a teenager, I truly obsessed about my weight. As a child, I ate regular meals and never worried about portions, calories, fat, or the like. However, I did eat a lot of sugar. Then as a teen, it seemed that all of a sudden I became self-conscious about my weight. It didn't help that one of my first boyfriends said to me, 'You're really ly cute, Julia, but you'd be a lot cuter if you lost ten pounds.' Of course I believed him, so the dieting began.

"I dieted, fasted (on diet soft drinks!), exercised compulsively, and some days I starved myself. I didn't eat when I was hungry, but sometimes I would stuff myself until I was nearly bursting. I had completely lost track of my natural hunger, but I didn't know it. When

I was 30, I reached a time of personal crisis in my life and made the decision to see a counselor. Not long after we began our sessions, I made the horrifying discovery that I had an eating disorder. I had denied myself good meals, but then I would eat three chocolate bars in one sitting. Or I would go to the store and buy a box of potato chips and some dip and eat it all at once, literally not being able to stop. It occurred to me that many other people did not eat this way.

"*I recognized that my weight problem stemmed from being sexually abused as a child. I was told by the abuser that this was happening to me because I was pretty. Since I learned that being pretty 'caused' the abuse, why would I want to be pretty? Gaining weight was a good way to stop being pretty. Also, I realized that eating and food were two things in my life I felt I could control. Because I had dealt with much of the pain regarding the sexual abuse, I knew it was time to close the door on the past and move forward with courage.*"

We'll come back to Julia's case when we remove the mask. How she released the weight she had been holding on to is an inspiring story.

In looking at the mask of the Obsessed, I asked myself if I had ever worn it, and I quickly heard the answer: "Your need to write is compulsive." I thought about this for a few moments and counted the books I had written—20 nonfiction books (including this one) and 5 novels in 19 years, plus more than 200 *Quartus Reports*. I realized something that had not occurred to me before. To write for the joy of it is fine; to want to contribute something to others as a way of service is altruistic. But to be *driven* by an activity to the extent that everything else becomes secondary is abnormal. So I had to take a good look at this obsessive behavior, and what came to the surface of my mind was a basic state of insecurity. On an unconscious level was the thought that if I didn't sit at the computer and write day after day, my prosperity would be limited. I was equating the books with financial security, and here was the man who had written *The Abundance Book*, which states that total dependance on Spirit is the key to abundant living. Oh my. We never know what may lurk in the subterranean regions of mind, so I was glad that this error pattern was revealed.

"Insecurity" had another face, too. It was the idea that I had to constantly prove to myself—and the readers—that I was good enough and knew enough to write spiritual literature. This wasn't humility; it was ego-arrogance—and by writing this chapter, I have been able to change my mind and find the mask slipping away. Let's get rid of that ugly disguise now, once and for all.

Removing the Mask

In the early part of this chapter, I quoted John Bradshaw as saying that at the root of obsessions lies shame. We should deal with that first, and Bradshaw's remedy in healing shame includes sharing our feelings with significant others. This means to come out of isolation and stop hiding from ourselves, and if we don't have a spouse or intimate relationship to help us heal our shame, then we should consider a support group. One thing I love about the Quartus gatherings is that we trust each other and can share together, give up our ego defenses, and face the demons within. You may also find other such groups in your church, or in the various 12-step programs. Just keep in mind that the purpose of this part of the healing process is to freely express your feelings to someone who is loving and nonjudgmental. As Bradshaw puts it, "The *only* way out of toxic shame is to embrace the shame."[2]

Now let's look at another factor that feeds the addictive personality. Whenever there are feelings of self-doubt, insecurity, inadequacy, unworthiness, and unfulfillment, they can be traced back to one single central life issue: *guilt*. Guilt screens out the free-flow of God's love in action, grace, the all-inclusive supply. When we feel guilty, we are not at peace, and the lack of peace brings forth desperation, which drives us to out-of-control urges.

What we feel guilty about are the mistakes we think we've made in the past—something we've done or haven't done—cheating, lying, stealing, hurting, or being vulnerable to others' abuse, manipulation, fanaticism, and meddling. We feel guilty for actions taken in anger, fear, and indifference, or for being weak, subservient, and under the control of others. It seems that the path of our lives is sprinkled with the sands of guilt.

To be free of guilt, we must choose freedom from guilt, and in doing so, we must understand that *we* decided to feel guilty in the first place. No one placed the guilt upon us. It is our creation, and we must realize that we are the ones responsible. Knowing this, we can now begin the healing process. Go back in time and write in your journal every experience, action, or situation in your life where there is any semblance of remorse, grief, or anguish. Be thorough and be honest. Look at the family environment, your school days, activities in the workplace, and interactions with people on every level. Describe every scenario in great detail. Begin as far back as you can remember, and follow the path all the way up to the present time.

Once you have completed this review in writing, go into meditation and touch that Light of the Presence within. Become one in consciousness with your Holy Self, and then take each point of self-reproach, one at a time, and *speak aloud* to the healing Light, saying what you did or didn't do with great feeling. Yes, this is a form of confession. Tell your Spirit everything, holding nothing back, and feel the forgiving-healing energy flowing through you. Give it all up to the Light, and see it dissolved in consciousness. Let the tears flow as part of the cleansing process, and know that Spirit loves you, has never condemned you, and with your willingness, will remove everything in mind and heart that is holding you back from living a rich, full, and joyful life.

Let the peace and love of God fill the vacuum that is left. Feel the peace. Feel the love, knowing that peace is the fountain and love is the living water that flows to connect heaven and earth. Now tear out the pages of guilt in your journal and burn them, and then let's meditate together.

I have released the past to the Presence of God within, and the stains have been removed. I am guiltless, innocent, and free.

I accept the peace and love of God, and know that the Universe approves of me. Therefore, I can approve of myself.

The illusions have been shattered, and my conscious awareness is now directed to the Holy Self I AM, the only Reality of my being.

And to my Self I say . . . I let your Mind be my mind, your Thoughts my thoughts, your Vision my vision, your Power my power. I seek nothing in this world, only your glorious expression through me.

I now rest in the Silence, listening to my Voice from on high.

In an Ageless Wisdom text we find . . .

By the development of goodwill, which is the will of good intentions and motive, will come the healing of . . . obsessions, and an attainment of equilibrium and of rhythm.[3]

Look at the key words: *goodwill, good intentions and motive, equilibrium, rhythm.* How do they resonate with your consciousness, your purpose in life, your way of living? Weave these characteristics into your thinking and feeling nature, and think on these thoughts with peace and love.

I am kind and compassionate.
My resolutions are on fire with inspiration.
I live with balance and in the natural flow of life.

I am not deceived by illusion.
I live in the Light of Reality.
My inner nature is freedom and joy.
I am willing to see all others recognize their freedom and joy.
The more I give of myself, the more I have to give.
I am no longer resistant to life.
All that is rightfully mine is drawn to me.
I live in bliss.

Now let's go back and look at Julia's story. Recall that she discovered she had an eating disorder, which she recognized as stemming from sexual abuse as a child. Again quoting from her letter:

"With great mortification, I joined Overeaters Anonymous [OA] and proclaimed myself a compulsive overeater. The blessing of this program is that it is based on spiritual principles. The first step was to admit that I was powerless over food, but that a Power greater than myself could take away my insanity. So I admitted this every day in my prayers and asked my Higher Power to take away my desire to eat compulsively and my desire for sugar, which I learned I was addicted to.

"It was at OA that I learned how to identify exactly when I was being compulsive. As I found out, it was not so much what I ate, but the state of mind, or the emotional state I was in while I ate it. It's actually possible to eat healthy food, such as fruit, compulsively. And eating a chocolate bar isn't 'bad.' It's when I absolutely HAD to eat it, or ate it feverishly, with no regard for what I was eating that made it compulsive. I began to realize that when feelings came up inside of me that I couldn't handle, I would reach for comfort food and stuff those feelings back down. It's the same way a drug addict reaches for a hit to numb the feelings he is experiencing.

"It was quite amazing that when I asked my Higher Power to take away my desire to eat compulsively and my desire for sugar, it was taken away almost immediately. Then once again I began to eat

compulsively and gained back all the weight I had lost. At that time. I honestly didn't care if I released the weight anymore and just thanked Spirit for my perfect body. And then something amazing happened. One day I looked in the mirror and thought, Am I slimmer? *I decided to weigh myself, thinking that maybe I had released five pounds. I was shocked when I saw the numbers on the scale. I had, in fact, released 15 pounds without even trying. When I became comfortable with my weight the way it was, and thanked Spirit for my perfect body, I released the weight I had been holding on to."*

Ponder this secret of dealing with your obsessions and their effects.

Let's return to the mythological picture—the woman stuffing her mouth with something in both hands, fear on her face, body trembling. The key words are: *"One can only heal the inner by gratifying the outer."* There's little symbolism here. It's an accurate portrait of ingestive addiction. For the other forms of obsession—yours, in particular—let the picture form on the screen of your mind, and sketch what you see.

In the process of removing the mask, you were motivated to share what may be considered your "shame" with someone you can trust. This was an important step. You also gave up your guilt through an emotionally stirring exercise, and were transformed in the Light. At that moment, you were no longer a captive of the ego. Actually, the reverse was true—you captured the lower nature through reuniting with your Source, and finding a means of escape was not a satisfactory solution anymore.

You have recognized the chains that bound you, have stopped resisting them, have thanked Spirit for a consciousness of wholeness and perfection—and you watched the obsessions melt away. Resignation and submissiveness to illusion and effects are no longer a part of your nature now. You realize you have a holy destiny, and you are determined to achieve it. Yes!

I feel that way, and you do, too. Together, we will let our masks fall away.

chapter
twelve

THE DECEIVER

To deceive is to cause someone to believe something that is not true. A Deceiver is one who is *intentionally* false, and behind that mask, we may find several other disguises in full support, such as the Manipulator, the Meddler, the Prideful, and the Obsessed—all mixed and mingled in a false face of dishonesty and deception.

> *"Deceivers are the most dangerous members of society.*
> *They trifle with the best affections of our nature,*
> *and violate the most sacred obligations."*
> — George Crabbe, English poet

> *"O, what a tangled web we weave,*
> *when first we practice to deceive."*
> — Walter Scott, Scottish novelist

In Revelations 12:9, the Devil and Satan are called "the deceivers of the whole world." Who is this Devil-Satan? The *Metaphysical Bible Dictionary* says this adversary "assumes various forms in man's consciousness, among which may be mentioned egotism, a puffing up of the personality; and the opposite of this, self-deprecation, which admits the 'accuser' into the consciousness. . . . Satan is the 'Devil,' a state of mind formed by man's personal ideas of his power and completeness and sufficiency apart from God."[1]

Yes, the adversary is none other than ego, that now familiar false self, a self-created entity or thought-form that is diametrically opposite of the True Self. It is an unconscious belief that we created ourselves, or that we were created exclusively as life-forms, as individuals, through a male-female fusion and a fertilized egg—that we are certainly not eternal living expressions of God. While you, as a spiritual aspirant, may not consider such thinking as coming from a sane mind, remember that each one of us is the sum-total of the contributing influences in life.

Accordingly, we see everything that happens to us and everyone we meet in the light of this "nature" that has been built up over the years. We identify ourselves as a persona (meaning a player's mask) through which we speak and act. And the difference between a normal and abnormal persona is the knowledge that Something within is greater than the mask. The more we separate ourselves from our Truth of being, the more insane we become—and the Deceiver is one of the greatest forms of madness. It is a consciousness that believes it alone is responsible for what happens in life, that the mask is supreme and spirituality is superstition, with a thought system that says, "I'll do whatever it takes to get what I want."

With that kind of attitude, everyone becomes either a potential or real enemy. In ego-consciousness we look at what our problem seems to be and place it on someone else, and the person receiving the projection is then to blame, which means he or she must be punished. The Deceiver sees everyone in this light, which leads to an inability to distinguish between right or wrong—and everyone becomes fair game.

In my early days struggling in the business world, I was certainly vulnerable to Deceivers. Nelson, a dyed-in-the-wool con man, I realized later, talked me into co-signing a note for a large loan that he said he needed to settle an estate in Louisiana. He got the money, thanked me, promptly left for Europe, and was never heard from again. Then there was Jerry. He said his mother was desperately ill in

New York and he needed money for the airfare. I gave it to him, and he vanished, too. I heard later from one of his friends that his mother had passed away the year before.

Debra married a Deceiver, but didn't know it until they combined their financial resources—she had a sizable inheritance, and he had very little—and he emptied out the bank accounts and left town. She still hasn't been able to find him. Eric was hired by an engineering firm—not based on his education or abilities—but as a strategy to influence Eric's father, who was awarding city contracts. Connie bought a brand-new car and later discovered it had been damaged, repaired, and sold as factory fresh.

People who fabricate stories to intentionally mislead are Deceivers, as are those who play a role to misrepresent themselves by appearing to be something they're not.

Put Deceivers together in a group and you have what Ancient Wisdom calls "organized evil." Think of the scams that are played out on the elderly to con them out of their life savings, the telemarketers who lie through their teeth to get your credit card numbers, and the unethical solicitations for money from so-called charitable groups whose only charity is themselves.

Looking at the planetary energies that influence the Deceiver consciousness—those with a vulnerability to the limiting aspects of the forces—we see that there is a strong desire for material power and a drive to have control over others. The individual is extremely self-ish, arrogant, ruthless, and totally self-centered, with no regard for anyone. There is great turmoil in mind, yet the person can be ingen-ious in double-dealing. He or she is the lone-wolf type, even when operating within a group of other Deceivers, and will possess an overestimation of personal abilities, usually to cover up a deep-seat-ed inferiority complex.

When the angel-archetypes within are repressed, great emphasis will be placed on purposely misleading people in order to get one's way. Lying will become a habit, second nature, and controlled visualization will be used to plot and plan nefarious deeds. Accomplishing goals will be done in the most expedient and unscrupulous way.

Edwin C. Steinbrecher, the noted metaphysical astrologer, says:

> Lying to yourself or to others confuses the archetypes which are creating and sustaining your reality. When they register your perceived outer reality in one way and then you define this same reality in an entirely different way by lying, two separate sets of instructions are received by them—two contradictory suggestions are made as to how to create your reality experience. These contradictions create imbalance, first in yourself, then in your outer reality, and imbalance generally brings with it pain or disease.[2]

The psychological profile of the Deceiver shows us that there is an essential disrespect for others. Failure in relationships and/or activities at an early age is translated into a belief that the person is a failure as a human being. Emptiness is then filled with envy. There may also be perceived barriers to upward mobility based on family environment, education, gender, or race. Also, the Deceiver personality can be developed as the result of limited social experience with the mother, and a lack of emotional security, with demands placed on the child that he or she felt couldn't be met.

Think of the Deceivers you've known, and look at the times when *you* wore that false face. What do you feel was the primary motivation for deception? It seems to me that the underlying emotion of the Deceiver is fear. Because of ego-dominance, the Deceiver is alone in the world, with no spiritual presence to rely on for guidance, safety, and protection—and the fear of this isolation continues to build.

Even those who are on the spiritual path can be "casually" deceptive, afraid of what might happen if the truth were told. And sometimes we become the great pretender to mask the fear, to disguise what's really going on in our lives. Have you done that? I have. I've tried to give the impression that I was very successful and financially fit when I wasn't—fearful of not getting new accounts if I didn't display an aura of true success. I look back now and see that I couldn't trust the universe, be myself, and draw forth the clients whom I could serve well and would compensate me accordingly.

Even when I once fell off an upper deck and broke my hip and pelvis, I deceived the doctors—lied about being able to walk on crutches with no pain so that I could limit my stay in the hospital. I told myself that I had to get out of there so that I could go home and experience a true healing. But I can also see now that I was afraid of the doctors and the environment of the hospital—I had never been confined in one. Yet I had written in *The Superbeings* that God works through physicians, which had to include *where* they were practicing.

In the Wisdom Teachings, it is written that the power of fear "is increased potently through the powers of the mind, through *memory* of past pain and grievance, and through anticipation of these . . . the power of fear is enormously aggravated by the thought-form we ourselves have built of our own individual fears and phobias. This thought-form grows in power as we pay attention to it, for 'energy follows thought,' till we become dominated by it."[3]

The "memory of past pain and grievance" is important here—not only in ourselves, but also what we may have inflicted on others. The boomerang comes back, we find ourselves in a similar situation, and we remember the past pain. So what do we do? We put on the mask of the Deceiver to make things right.

Through a third party, I heard about Ray. He had been divorced twice, with his mother "raising hell" with him both times—she felt it had to be his fault. When his third wife walked out on him, he began to play the role (for his mother's benefit) of the indignant, shocked, and disgusted husband—the faithful one who had caught his wife in bed with another man. It was a lie, of course, but suddenly—in his mother's eyes—Ray was the courageous soul who stood strong and righted a wrong. Mama was proud. Ray was smiling, feeling good.

That lasted until the mother had a chance encounter with her former daughter-in-law.

The mythological picture of the extreme Deceiver shows us a head of a man with the body of a spider in a web. One side of the face appears "good"—smiling with a sympathetic eye. The other side of the face is evil—anger on the mouth, hate in the eye. The key words are: *"Duplicity is my chosen path."* Sketch what you see in your journal.

The picture I saw in my pretending days was me with my hand behind my back, fingers crossed. What do you see for yourself?

Removing the Mask

We have seen that the Deceiver mask is a fearful one, so the first thing you should do is address your fears. I've asked this before, and it's worth repeating. What are you afraid of? To be fearful is to be pessimistic about life, which is the epitome of the Deceiver mask. And what is the other side of the coin? *Optimism.* Garret Condon wrote in the *Hartford Courant* that "researchers at the Mayo Clinic in Rochester, Minnesota, have confirmed what many people already believe: Optimists tend to live longer, healthier lives."

Condon goes on to quote psychologist Michael Mercer as saying that "optimism is a habit that can be acquired. . . .He encourages people to concentrate on what they want in life, not what they don't want. Optimists, he said, focus on solutions rather than problems. In other words, switch from 'I hate my boss' to 'What can I do to build my career?' Once people decide what whey want, they should spend more than half their time pursuing their goals."[4]

What do *you* want in life? How would you describe an *ideal* life? If you are like most people I've spoken to about this, it would include harmonious relationships, financial self-sufficiency, wholeness in mind and body, and a sense of accomplishment through inspired creative activities. The Deceiver may also want this, but it is all to be achieved through duplicity, for to this individual, that is the only way. For those on the spiritual path, however, we recognize that such ideals—as the Will of God in expression—represent effects, and to have this measure of heaven on earth, we must look to Cause. And when we focus our minds on the Source within and the opportunities that are ours through the activity of Spirit, we are not only optimistic, we are ecstatic over our unlimited potential in life. But to reach that state of being, we need to get rid of the fears.

Open your journal now and make a list of what you consider threatening or intimidating in your life. After you do so, look at the list and realize why you're fearful. It's because you do not fully trust God. So what's the answer? Simply put, a change in attitude—to switch the focus of mind from personality to Individuality, from ego to Spirit. Spirit within is God being you. It is a living, pulsating, shining, all-knowing, all-powerful Divine Consciousness embodying the fullness of Father-Mother God *as* your Essential Self. It is *you*. It is the *I* that you are, and there is nothing It cannot do.

Now think of your personality as the instrument, the channel, for this Force-for-Good. Your mind is the transmitter of the divine energies that comprise "heaven," which flow through you to manifest as form and experience on the earth plane. When there is fear, the channel for expression is closed, but the fear can be dissolved through love—by realizing God's love for you.

God has never condemned you, recognizes no sin, is incapable of unforgiveness, and is an ever-present help at every moment in time and space. Look at the Prodigal Son and the Father's rejoicing over his return, embracing him with love and calling for a celebration. God's love does not have to be earned; it is infinite and forever in expression.

Choose to accept God's love now, and open your heart to receive it. As you feel the blazing light of that love enter your heart-center, know that it is also flowing down through the other chakras to eliminate the darkness of fear, anger, envy, jealousy, and insecurity. Perfect love casts out all fear—and everything related to it.

Let's work with this meditation. Turn within and say:

> *I choose to believe that God loves me.*
>
> *I choose to accept God's love for me now.*
>
> *I am grateful for that love, and within the depths of my being, I understand that regardless of what I have ever thought, said, or done, that love has never diminished. God's love for me is continuous and complete.*
>
> *I rest in the silence in God's love, knowing that it is enfolding me and lifting me up to show me that I am worthy of this love.*
>
> *I am beginning to love myself as never before.*

Now let's look at faith. If your consciousness is filled with fear and anxiety, that is where your faith is. You are putting your faith in the possibility and probability of misfortune, lack, and limitation. Your consciousness, which is your faith, your substance, must by law act upon itself. Your faith vibration attracts what you have and experience in this world because like attracts like. How much faith do you have? Look at your life. Jesus said that if your faith was no larger than a mustard seed, you could level a mountain. So the secret is to become aware that you already possess the faith necessary to do all things. Let's fan that spark with this meditation.

> *I believe that there is nothing God cannot do. I believe there is nothing God cannot do through me. I believe there is nothing God cannot do as me. God is my Holy Self; therefore, there is nothing I cannot do. Nothing is too good for God, and nothing is too good for me.*
>
> *I love the faith I am with all my heart, and I draw forth the omnipotence of this incredible energy and experience it now filling my feeling nature with its awesome power. My*

*emotions are saturated with total trust, total certainty, and
total conviction in myself as a dynamic expression of God.*

At this point, think of the personality that you present to the
world, and contemplate these thoughts:

> *I am a spiritual being.*
> *I am loved.*
> *I am filled with the power of faith.*
> *I have self-respect.*
> *I have integrity.*
> *I have patience.*
> *I am willing to learn.*
> *I am caring.*
> *I enjoy helping others.*
> *I use my energies wisely.*
> *Love is more important than my desires.*
> *I seek the high road in life.*

Since the ego is the Deceiver, another way to remove the mask is
to have a particular angel-archetype within take the place of the ego
until that misqualified energy has been transmuted. I'm referring to
the Angel of Truth and Enlightenment, a living energy that has been
called the Higher Self, the manifest Christ, and the Jesus archetype.
It is an extension of your very Spirit, a dynamic ray from the central
Sun within. The key here is to become *consciously* one with this
power within and let it be the primary light of the personality.

Those of you who have read *The Angels Within Us* know how to
make contact with this archetype. Ask your spirit guide to escort you
into deep inner space, and at a certain point, you will see the angel's
light. As you draw close to it, notice as the light begins to take on the
form and appearance of a physical being. Tell the angel that it is your
intention to bond consciously with him (the energy has a masculine
quality) so that he may take the place of the ego. Then with purpose

of mind, see this Angel of Truth and Enlightenment merge fully with your being. Feel the unity. See the light of Truth spreading throughout your being, and identify your thinking-feeling personality with the shining Sun of God. As you continue working with this process, a completely different vibration will take place in your force field, and as you go back into the world, you will do so—not as a Deceiver—but as the living Truth.

Recall the mythological picture—the head of a man with facial expressions of good and evil and with the body of a spider in a web. The key words are: *"Duplicity is my chosen path."* If we properly interpret the facial expression, we see that he is saying, "Trust me, and let me have what I want because I'm going to get it anyway." He thinks you're a dupe, a fool, an easy mark, and he's going to have his way with you. The spider and the web are symbolic of a secret snare, a trap being laid through stealth. This is a most vivid portrait of a hardened Deceiver. If a less extreme picture comes to mind, one that would best describe the mask as you've worn it, sketch it in your journal.

Understand that as you remove *your* masks, you are no longer vulnerable to the false faces of others. As we have seen, the Deceivers out there are looking for the Victim, the Abandoned, the Worrier, the Yielder, and the Prideful—and they can spot them in a minute. But when they see you with poise, power, confidence, and self-worth radiating from your consciousness, they'll know that they've met their match. They will flee back into the darkness from which they came, eventually to see the light and remove the mask that binds them to the lower world.

Without your disguises, your role in the scheme of things now is simply to be the shining Sun of Truth you are. Remember what Jesus said, as recorded in the *Pistis Sophia Treatise of the Gnostics:*

Know ye not and do ye not understand that ye are all Angels, all Archangels, Gods and Lords, all Rulers, all the great Invisibles, all those of the Midst, those of every region of them that are on the Right, all the Great Ones of the emanations of the Light with all their glory . . .[5]

Can you accept the Truth that the Crowning Glory of Creation was not a race of human beings, but Beings of Light—Spiritual Beings, Divine Individuals fully ordained as Holy Ones of the Most High? As you do, all masks will fall, and you will reveal yourself as the very Face of God being *You*.

And to your brothers and sisters walking the Path, you will say: *I see you*. And they will respond: *I am here*.

NOTES

CHAPTER TWO
1. John Randolph Price, *A Spiritual Philosophy for the New World* (Carlsbad, CA: Hay House, Inc., 1997), pp. 52–53.

CHAPTER THREE
1. John Randolph Price, *The Alchemist's Handbook* (Carlsbad, CA: Hay House, Inc., 2000).

CHAPTER FOUR
1. John Randolph Price, *The Abundance Book* (Carlsbad, CA: Hay House, Inc., 1996), pp. 21–24.
2. ——, *The Jesus Code* (Carlsbad, CA: Hay House, Inc., 2000), p. 72.

CHAPTER FIVE
1. John Randolph Price, *A Spiritual Philosophy for the New World* (Carlsbad, CA: Hay House, Inc., 1997), p. 94.
2. ——, *Empowerment* (Carlsbad, CA: Hay House, Inc., 1996), pp. 45–46.
3. ——, *The Jesus Code* (Carlsbad, CA: Hay House, Inc., 2000), p. 103.
4. H. Emilie Cady, *Lessons in Truth* (Unity Village, MO: Unity Books, 1894), pp. 93–94.

CHAPTER SIX

1. *San Antonio Express-News*, October 31, 1999 (9A), "FBI fears Y2K violence"—as reported by David A. Vise and Lorraine Adams in the *Washington Post*.

2. *Time* magazine, January 12, 1999, p. 70.

3. Ibid., p. 67.

4. *San Antonio Express-News*, May 30, 1991; Rev. Don Baugh's column (B7)—"Looking for life's spiritual signs."

5. John Randolph Price, *The Angels Within Us* (New York: Fawcett Columbine/Ballantine, 1993), p. 226.

6. Kenneth Wapnick, *Forgiveness and Jesus* (Roscoe, NY: Foundation for "A Course in Miracles," 1983), p. 34.

7. Ibid., pp. 37–38.

8. Alice A. Bailey, *Discipleship in the New Age* (New York: Lucis Publishing Company, 1972), p. 245.

9. John Randolph Price, *The Jesus Code* (Carlsbad, CA: Hay House, Inc., 2000), p. 133.

10. *A Course in Miracles*, Vol. I, Text (Tiburon, CA: Foundation for Inner Peace, 1975), p. 92.

11. John Randolph Price, *With Wings As Eagles* (Carlsbad, CA: Hay House, Inc., 1997), pp. 85–88.

CHAPTER SEVEN

1. Louise L. Hay and Friends, *Millennium 2000: A Positive Approach* (Carlsbad, CA: Hay House, Inc., 1999), pp. 138–139.

2. Alice A. Bailey, *Esoteric Healing* (New York: Lucis Publishing Company, 1953), pp. 69–70.

3. John Randolph Price, *The Jesus Code* (Carlsbad, CA: Hay House Inc., 2000), p. 73.

4. Ibid., pp. 74, 77.

5. John Randolph Price, *The Angels Within Us* (New York: Fawcett Columbine/Ballantine, 1993), pp. 289–290.

6. John Randolph Price, *Living a Life of Joy* (New York: Fawcett Columbine/Ballantine, 1997), pp. 48–49.

CHAPTER EIGHT

1. Louise L. Hay, *You Can Heal Your Life* (Carlsbad, CA: Hay House, Inc., 1984), p. 69.
2. John Randolph Price, *The Jesus Code* (Carlsbad, CA: Hay House, Inc., 2000), pp. 127–128.
3. Suzanne E. Harrill, *Affirm Yourself Day By Day* (Houston, TX: Innerworks Publishing, 1991), January 3—Worthiness.
4. Ibid., January 5—Unconditional Love.
5. John Randolph Price, *A Spiritual Philosophy for the New World* (Carlsbad, CA: Hay House, Inc., 1997), p. 3.
6. Sondra Ray, *Loving Relationships* (Millbrae, CA: Celestial Arts, 1980), p. 28.
7. Ibid., p. 76.

CHAPTER NINE

1. Carolyn Myss, *Anatomy of the Spirit* (New York: Harmony Books, a division of Crown Publishers, 1996), p. 129.
2. John Randolph Price, *The Angels Within Us* (New York: Fawcett Columbine/Ballantine, 1993), p. 96.
3. Isabel M. Hickey, *Astrology A Cosmic Science* (Sebastopol, CA: CRCS Publications, 1992), pp. 167–168.
4. Carolyn Myss, *Anatomy of the Spirit* (New York: Harmony Books, a division of Crown Publishers, 1996), p. 131.
5. Alice A. Bailey, *Esoteric Healing* (New York: Lucis Publishing Company, 1953), p. 569.

CHAPTER TEN

1. John Randolph Price, *The Jesus Code* (Carlsbad, CA: Hay House, Inc., 2000), p. 101.
2. Ibid., p. 102.
3. John Randolph Price, *The Angels Within Us* (New York: Fawcett Columbine/Ballantine, 1993), pp. 217–218.
4. Louise L. Hay, *You Can Heal Your Life* (Carlsbad, CA: Hay House, Inc., 1984), p. 84.

CHAPTER ELEVEN

1. John Bradshaw, *Healing the Shame That Binds You* (Deerfield Beach, FL: Health Communications, Inc., 1988), p. 15.
2. Ibid., p. 120.
3. Alice A. Bailey, *Esoteric Healing* (New York: Lucis Publishing Company, 1953), p. 108.

CHAPTER TWELVE

1. *Metaphysical Bible Dictionary* (Unity Village, MO: Unity School of Christianity, 1931), p. 575.
2. Edwin C. Steinbrecher, *The Inner Guide Meditation* (York Beach, ME: Samuel Weiser, Inc., 1988), p. 177.
3. Alice A. Bailey, *A Treatise on White Magic* (New York: Lucis Publishing Company, 1967), p. 238.
4. *San Antonio Express-News*, February 14, 2000 (4D), "Optimists tend to live longer"—as reported by Garret Condon in the *Hartford Courant*.
5. G.R.S. Mead, *Fragments of a Faith Forgotten* (Hyde Park, NY: University Books, n.n.), pp. 487–488.

ABOUT THE AUTHOR

John Randolph Price, bestselling author, lecturer, and workshop facilitator, has devoted more than 30 years to researching Ancient Wisdom and tracing the Golden Cord of the philosophic mysteries through the centuries. He has combined this material with modern metaphysics and spiritual psychology in the writing of his many books.

In 1981, he and his wife, Jan, formed The Quartus Foundation, a spiritual research and communications organization. For information about workshops, the annual Mystery School conducted by John and Jan Price, and their monthly publications, please contact:

The Quartus Foundation
P.O. Box 1768
Boerne, TX 78006
(830) 249-3985 • (830) 249-3318 (fax)
E-mail: quartus@texas.net
Website: quartus.org

We hope you enjoyed this Hay House book.
If you would like to receive a free catalog featuring additional
Hay House books and products, or if you would like information
about the Hay Foundation, please contact:

HAY
HOUSE

Hay House, Inc.
P.O. Box 5100
Carlsbad, CA 92018-5100

(760) 431-7695 or **(800) 654-5126**
(760) 431-6948 (fax) or **(800) 650-5115 (fax)**

Please visit the Hay House Website at: **hayhouse.com**